Program Administration Scale

Measuring Early Childhood Leadership and Management

TEACHERS COLLEGE PRESS

Teachers College,
Columbia University
New York and London

Teri N. Talan, M.Ed., J.D. *and*

Paula Jorde Bloom, Ph.D.

Published by Teachers College Press, 1234 Amsterdam Avenue, New York, NY 10027

ISBN 978-0-8077-4528-1

Printed on acid-free paper
Manufactured in the United States of America

11   10   8   7

Training is available from the McCormick Tribune Center for Early Childhood Leadership for practitioners, researchers, and program evaluators to help ensure the most reliable use of the *Program Administration Scale*. Contact Teri Talan, the McCormick Tribune Center for Early Childhood Leadership, National-Louis University, 6310 Capitol Drive, Wheeling, Illinois 60090, 800/443-5522, ext. 5060 or ttalan@nl.edu for further information.

Contents

Acknowledgments

The impetus for the *Program Administration Scale* (PAS) came from our work assessing program quality as part of a McCormick Tribune Foundation professional development initiative. The experience convinced us of the need for a valid and reliable instrument to measure the quality of leadership and management practices of center-based early care and education programs. The W. Clement and Jessie V. Stone Foundation provided the funding to conduct the reliability and validity study of the PAS. We are indebted to both foundations for their support of our work and for their commitment to improving the quality of early childhood program administration.

We are deeply appreciative of the insights we received from experts in the field who helped shape the development of the *Program Administration Scale*. Our heartfelt thanks go to Kay Albrecht, Bee Jay Ciszek, Doug Clark, Dick Clifford, Debby Cryer, Eileen Eisenberg, Jana Fleming, Lois Gamble, John Gunnarson, Thelma Harms, Judy Harris Helm, Kendra Kett, Stacy Kim, Jackie Legg, Sam Meisels, Anne Mitchell, Gwen Morgan, Kathie Raiborn, Susan Sponheimer, Marilyn Sprague-Smith, and Lana Weiner. We also benefitted from our discussions with the National Association for the Education of Young Children (NAEYC) Program Administration Standards Technical Review Team under the leadership of Stacie Goffin, Linda Espinosa, and Barbara Smith.

Appreciation also goes to the research team involved in the reliability and validity study of the PAS: Linda Butkovich, Lisa Downey, Shirley Flath, Kathy Hardy, Karen May, Gale Reinitz, Sara Starbuck, and Cass Wolfe. Jan Maruna and the staff of the Illinois Network of Child Care Resource and Referral Agencies (INCCRRA) were particularly helpful during the sample selection process. A special thank you to the early childhood administrators who graciously gave their time and welcomed our research team into their centers.

We are grateful to the statisticians at the Metropolitan Chicago Information Center (MCIC) who assisted with the data analysis, to Jan Perney for his review of the manuscript, and to Donna Jonas for her assistance in preparing the final document. And finally, we are especially indebted to Jill Bella, our colleague at the McCormick Tribune Center for Early Childhood Leadership, whose support and technical assistance were invaluable during all phases of the development of this instrument.

Overview of the Program Administration Scale

Rationale

The genesis of the *Program Administration Scale* (PAS) was the growing professional consensus that early childhood program quality should be viewed through a broader lens than only that of the classroom learning environment, and that it should incorporate multi-source data collection methods including interview, document review, and observation. While there are several instruments available to measure the quality of teacher–child interactions and the quality of the classroom instructional practices, there does not currently exist a valid and reliable instrument that solely measures the administrative practices of an early childhood program. The *Program Administration Scale* was designed to fill that void. (See Psychometric Characteristics of the PAS on pages 69–73.)

Research has consistently found that overall administrative practices are crucial for ensuring high-quality outcomes for children and families (Bloom, 1989, 1996a, 1996b; Cost, Quality, and Child Outcomes Study Team, 1995; Kagan & Bowman, 1997; Phillips, Mekos, Scarr, McCartney, & Abbott-Shim, 2000; Whitebook, Howes, & Phillips, 1990). Without quality systems in place at the organizational level, high-quality interactions and learning environments at the classroom level cannot be sustained.

The *Program Administration Scale* (PAS) was designed to serve as a reliable and easy-to-administer tool for measuring the overall quality of administrative practices of early care and education programs and as a useful guide to improve programs. The development of the PAS began with a review of the literature on best practices in management and early childhood program quality, with an eye to organizational practices that foster collaboration, diversity, cultural sensitivity, and social justice.

The instrument includes 25 items clustered in 10 subscales that measure both leadership and management functions of center-based early childhood programs. Leadership functions relate to the broad view of helping an organization clarify and affirm values, set goals, articulate a vision, and chart a course of action to achieve that vision. Management functions relate to the actual orchestration of tasks and the setting up of systems to carry out the organizational mission (Bloom, 2003).

Designed for early childhood program administrators, researchers, monitoring personnel, and quality enhancement facilitators, the PAS was constructed to complement the widely used observation-based classroom environment rating scales designed by Harms, Clifford, and Cryer (1998, 2003). Both the PAS and the environment rating scales (ECERS-R, ITERS-R) measure quality on a 7-point scale and both generate a profile to guide program improvement efforts. If used together, these instruments provide a focused look at best practices at the classroom level and the broad view of program quality from an organizational perspective.

Multi-Use Design

The *Program Administration Scale* is applicable for multiple uses: program self-improvement, technical assistance and monitoring, training, research and evaluation, and public awareness. Although the target audience for the PAS is center-based early care and education programs, the instrument is also appropriate for measuring and improving quality in public school-based programs.

- **Program Self-Improvement.** Because indicators are objective and quantifiable on a 7-point continuum from inadequate to excellent, center directors can easily set program goals to incrementally improve administrative practices. The resulting profile can be used to benchmark a center's progress in meeting those goals over time.

- **Technical Assistance and Monitoring.** As part of local or state quality-enhancement initiatives, the PAS can serve as a convenient technical assistance and monitoring tool, providing clear guidelines for incrementally improving organizational practices to ensure high-quality programming for children and families.

- **Training.** For both preservice and in-service training for program administrators, the PAS provides a broad overview of organizational practices, highlighting best practices in leadership and management, and reinforcing the important role that center directors play in shaping program quality.

- **Research and Evaluation.** For independent research studies or publicly funded, tiered-reimbursement initiatives that reward higher levels of program quality, the PAS can be used to describe current levels of program quality as well as benchmark change in pretest-posttest evaluation designs.

- **Public Awareness.** Because the PAS is written in clear language and provides a rubric of concrete examples of different leadership and management practices, it can help inform a wide range of stakeholders—center directors, agency administrators, state policymakers, licensing representatives, teacher trainers, parents, and resource and referral specialists—about the components of high-quality programming.

Subscales, Items, and Indicators

As explained earlier, the PAS measures quality on a 7-point scale in 25 items clustered in 10 subscales. The first 23 items relate to all programs. The last two items (24. Teacher and 25. Apprentice Teacher/Aide) are optional items depending on the program's staffing pattern. Each item is comprised of 2–5 indicator strands, and each indicator strand is scored on a 7-point scale from inadequate to excellent.

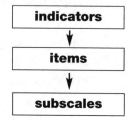

The following is a description of the subscales into which the items are grouped:

- **Human Resources Development** assesses whether the program provides an orientation for new staff, ongoing staff development, regular opportunities for supervision and support, and systematic performance appraisal.

- **Personnel Cost and Allocation** looks at whether the organization has a written salary scale and annual salary increases, the type and availability of fringe benefits, whether children are regrouped during the day to maintain ratios, and the availability of paid planning time for teaching staff.

- **Center Operations** considers the health and safety of the facility, whether the center has a risk-management plan, the adequacy of the space to meet the needs of staff, and the frequency and quality of internal communications including staff meetings and dispute resolution.

- **Child Assessment** examines the availability of screening procedures for identifying and referring children with special needs, the type and frequency of child assessments to determine child outcomes, and if the results of child assessments are used in curriculum planning and program evaluation.

- **Fiscal Management** looks at the director's role in the annual budget planning process, if payroll and other expenses are paid in a timely manner, and if standard accounting procedures are adhered to.

- **Program Planning and Evaluation** assesses whether the center has a written mission and vision statement, engages in strategic planning, and involves staff and parents in evaluating program practices.

- **Family Partnerships** examines the type and frequency of communication with parents, their level of involvement in center activities and decision making, and the degree of support the center provides to parents from different cultural and linguistic backgrounds.

- **Marketing and Public Relations** evaluates the type and frequency of different external communication tools, how responsive the center is to the needs of the neighborhoodor local community, and the administrator's involvement in civic, business, and early childhood professional organizations.

- **Technology** looks at the center's technological resources, the level of use of different software applications, and access to and level of use of the Internet by administrative and teaching staff.

- **Staff Qualifications** considers the level of general education, specialized training, and job experience of the on-site program administrator and members of the teaching staff.

Definition of Terms

The following definitions should be used in completing the PAS:

Administrator	The individual located on-site who is responsible for planning, implementing, and evaluating an early care and education program. Role titles for the administrator vary and include director, manager, and principal. This instrument does not include assessment of other administrative roles such as assistant director or education coordinator.
Lead Teacher	The individual with the highest educational qualifications assigned to teach a group of children and who is responsible for daily lesson planning, parent conferences, child assessment, and curriculum planning. This individual may also supervise other members of the teaching team. In some settings, this person is called a head teacher, master teacher, or teacher.
Teacher	A member of the teaching team who shares responsibility with the Lead Teacher for the care and education of an assigned group of children.
Apprentice Teacher/Aide	A member of the teaching team assigned to a group of children who works under the direct supervision of the Lead Teacher and/or Teacher.
sh	Semester hours of credit
ECE/CD	Early childhood education or child development

Using the PAS

Data-Collection Procedures

The *Program Administration Scale* was designed for use by program administrators as well as by trained independent assessors such as researchers, consultants, and program evaluators. The independent assessor using the PAS should schedule approximately two hours for an interview with the on-site administrator and an additional hour for a review of required documents. In advance of the visit, it is recommended that the administrator be provided with a copy of the *Program Administration Scale* and a list of the documents needed for review.

Upon arriving for the interview, the assessor should first ask the administrator for a brief tour of the facility, including the indoor and outdoor play environments, and any space specifically designated for families and staff. Observations of the facility are needed to complete the rating of two items (Item 7. Facilities Management and Item 20. Technological Resources). For the indicators needing documentation, the assessor should record a preliminary rating based on statements made by the administrator during the interview and the presence of the required documents. After the interview, a thorough review of the content of the documents should be conducted and adjustments made to the rating of the indicators if necessary.

For Items 1–21, questions are provided to guide the rating of the indicators. These questions can be found on the page facing the scoring page for each item. Independent assessors should use the questions to elicit information from the administrator during the interview. Center directors can also use these questions as prompts for rating the indicators.

Scoring the PAS

Adhering to the following two scoring principles for the *Program Administration Scale* will ensure the accuracy of the PAS profile and promote consistency in scoring across programs.

- In order to provide an accurate snapshot of program administrative practices, it is important that ratings be based only on the indicators provided for each item. For some indicators, scores are based solely on the administrator's self-report (e.g., Item 6. Staffing Patterns and Scheduling, Indicator 3.1). However, for most indicators, it is necessary to review documents or make observations in order to verify the accuracy of the information provided by the administrator. **For these verifiable indicators, a "D" (document) or an "O" (observation) appears under the indicator number** (e.g., Item 6. Staffing Patterns and Scheduling, Indicator 5.1).

- Scores should be based on existing policies and procedures, not past practices or plans for the future.

The following protocol should be used to score the *Program Administration Scale*:

Step 1. Rate the indicators for Items 1–21.

Use the following rules for rating the indicators:

- For each item, begin with the indicators under the 1 (inadequate) category and progress across the continuum of quality for each indicator to 7 (excellent), writing in the spaces provided a Y (yes) or N (no) if each indicator level applies.

- A rating of N/A (not applicable) may be given for indicators or for entire items when "N/A is allowed" is shown on the scale. Indicators rated N/A are not counted when determining the score for an item, and items scored N/A are not counted when calculating the Total PAS Score.
- Record supporting evidence in the box provided for comments (e.g., a document meets the criteria specified or an observation is made).

Step 2. Determine the scores for Items 1–21.

Use the following scoring rules for determining the item scores:

- A score of 1 is given if any indicator under the 1 column is rated Y (yes).
- A score of 2 is given when all indicators under 1 are rated N (no) and at least half of the indicators under 3 are rated Y (yes).
- A score of 3 is given when all indicators under 1 are rated N (no) and all indicators under 3 are rated Y (yes).
- A score of 4 is given when all indicators under 1 are rated N (no), all indicators under 3 are rated Y (yes), and at least half of the indicators under 5 are rated Y (yes).
- A score of 5 is given when all indicators under 1 are rated N (no), and all indicators under 3 and 5 are rated Y (yes).
- A score of 6 is given when all indicators under 1 are rated N (no), all the indicators under 3 and 5 are rated Y (yes), and at least half of the indicators under 7 are rated Y (yes).
- A score of 7 is given when all indicators under 1 are rated N (no) and all indicators under 3, 5, and 7 are rated Y (yes).

Circle the item score in the space provided in the lower right-hand corner on each item page.

Personnel Cost and Allocation

4. Compensation

1	2	3	4	5	6	7
Inadequate		Minimal		Good		Excellent

N 1.1 A written salary scale is not available.

Y 3.1 There is a written salary scale and it is available to
D some center staff.

N 5.1 A written salary scale is
D available to all center staff.*

Y 7.1 The salary scale is reviewed
D at least every three years for internal and external equity.**

N 1.2 A salary scale is based on role without regard to education and specialized training. ***

Y 3.2 Salary scale is differentiated
D by role, education, and specialized training.***

Y 5.2 Salary scale is differentiated
D by role, education, specialized training, and years of relevant experience.***

Y 7.2 Staff with comparable
D education, specialized training, and experience are paid comparable wages for comparable work.***

N 1.3 Staff did not receive a salary increase within the last two years.

Y 3.3 Staff received a salary
D increase within the last two years.

Y 5.3 Staff received an annual
D salary increase in each of the last three years.

N 7.3 The center has a compensation
D plan that provides for merit increases in addition to annual salary increases.

Comments:

Salary Scale available only to managers

Circle the final score based on the scoring rules on page 5.

1   2   3   (4)   5   6   7

4. Compensation

5

Step 3. Determine the scores for Items 22–25.
Complete the **Administrator Qualifications Worksheet** (page 62). Only one person is designated as the Administrator.

- Use this information to rate the indicators for Item 22. Administrator.
- Follow the scoring rules provided in Steps 1 and 2.

Complete a **Teaching Staff Qualifications Worksheet** (page 63) for each group of children, duplicating the form as needed.

- For scoring the PAS, it is necessary to designate as the Lead Teacher one of the adults who are responsible for the care and education of an assigned group of children. The Lead Teacher is the individual with the highest educational qualifications.
- Designate any other member of the teaching team who shares responsibility with the Lead Teacher for the care and education of an assigned group of children as a Teacher.
- Designate any member of the teaching team who works under the direct supervision of the Lead Teacher and/or Teacher as an Apprentice Teacher/Aide.
- Not all centers will have a staffing pattern that includes Teachers and/or Apprentice Teachers/Aides.
- Use the information from the **Teaching Staff Qualifications Worksheet** to rate the indicators for Item 23. Lead Teacher, Item 24. Teacher, and Item 25. Apprentice Teacher/Aide.
- Duplicate sufficient copies of Items 23, 24, and 25 so that the qualifications of each member of the teaching staff can be rated separately.
- Follow the rules provided in Steps 1 and 2.

Complete the **Summary of Teaching Staff Qualifications** (page 64).

- Transfer the individual item scores for each member of the teaching staff to the **Summary of Teaching Staff Qualifications**.
- Use the qualifications of the Lead Teachers assigned to each group of children to compute the Item 23 Average Score. Round this score to the closest whole number and enter on the **Item Summary Form** (page 65) for Item 23.
- Use the qualifications of any Teachers assigned to each group of children to compute the Item 24 Average Score. Round this score to the closest whole number and enter on the **Item Summary Form** for Item 24.
- Use the qualifications of any Apprentice Teachers/Aides assigned to each group of children to compute the Item 25 Average Score. Round this score to the closest whole number and enter on the **Item Summary Form** for Item 25.

Step 4. Generate a Total PAS Score.
The Total PAS Score is the sum of the item scores. To calculate this score, transfer the individual item scores to the **Item Summary Form** on page 65. Sum the item scores for the entire scale.

- If the program has a staffing pattern that includes Teachers **and** Apprentice Teachers/Aides, then 25 items are rated and the possible range of scores is 25–175.
- If the program has a staffing pattern that includes Teachers **or** Apprentice Teachers/Aides, then 24 items are rated and the possible range of scores is 24–168.
- If the program has a staffing pattern that does **not** include Teachers or Apprentice Teachers/Aides, then 23 items are rated and the possible range of scores is 23–161.

Step 5. Determine the Average PAS Item Score.

Use the **Item Summary Form** to calculate the Average PAS Item Score, which is the Total PAS Score divided by the number of items scored (a minimum of 23 for all programs; 24 or 25 for programs that have a staffing pattern that includes Teachers and/or Apprentice Teachers/Aides).

Step 6. Plot scores on the PAS Profile.

Plot the individual item scores on the graph of the **PAS Profile** on page 66; then connect the dots. Add the information at the bottom of the profile regarding the Total PAS Score, number of items scored, and Average PAS Item Score.

Item Summary Form

Program name: _Anywhere Child Care Center_   Date: ___8/15/04___

Instructions

Use this form to summarize the item scores and to calculate the Total PAS Score and Average PAS Item Score.

- Enter the item scores to the space provided.
- Sum all the item scores and enter the total in the space provided. This is the Total PAS Score
- Divide the Total PAS Score by the total number of items (minimum of 23 for all programs; 24 or 25 for programs that have a staffing pattern that includes Teachers and/or Apprentice Teachers/Aides). The resulting number is the Average PAS Item Score.

Item	Score
1. Staff Orientation	3
2. Supervision and Performance Appraisal	5
3. Staff Development	4
4. Compensation	4
5. Benefits	6
6. Staffing Patterns and Scheduling	2
7. Facilities Management	4
8. Risk Management	4
9. Internal Communications	5
10. Screening and Identification	6
11. Assessment in Support of Learning	5
12. Budget Planning	4
13. Accounting Practices	5
14. Program Evaluation	6
15. Strategic Planning	3
16. Family Communications	5
17. Family Support and Involvement	6
18. External Communications	3
19. Community Outreach	4
20. Technological Resources	3
21. Use of Technology	3
22. Administrator	3
23. Lead Teacher	4
24. Teacher	NA
25. Apprentice Teacher/Aide	2

Sum of item scores

99	÷	24	=	4.13
Total PAS Score		Number of items scored		Average PAS Item Score

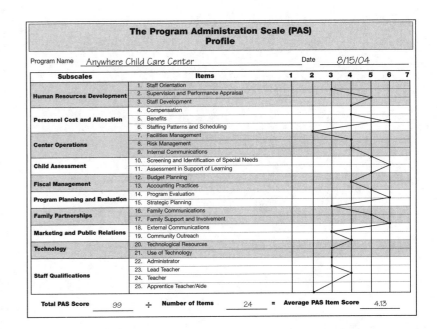

The Program Administration Scale (PAS) Profile

Program Name _Anywhere Child Care Center_   Date ___8/15/04___

Subscales	Items	1	2	3	4	5	6	7
Human Resources Development	1. Staff Orientation							
	2. Supervision and Performance Appraisal							
	3. Staff Development							
Personnel Cost and Allocation	4. Compensation							
	5. Benefits							
	6. Staffing Patterns and Scheduling							
Center Operations	7. Facilities Management							
	8. Risk Management							
	9. Internal Communications							
Child Assessment	10. Screening and Identification of Special Needs							
	11. Assessment in Support of Learning							
Fiscal Management	12. Budget Planning							
	13. Accounting Practices							
Program Planning and Evaluation	14. Program Evaluation							
	15. Strategic Planning							
Family Partnerships	16. Family Communications							
	17. Family Support and Involvement							
Marketing and Public Relations	18. External Communications							
	19. Community Outreach							
Technology	20. Technological Resources							
	21. Use of Technology							
Staff Qualifications	22. Administrator							
	23. Lead Teacher							
	24. Teacher							
	25. Apprentice Teacher/Aide							

Total PAS Score ___99___ ÷ **Number of Items** ___24___ = **Average PAS Item Score** ___4.13___

Program Administration Scale

Subscales and Items

Human Resources Development

1. Staff Orientation
2. Supervision and Performance Appraisal
3. Staff Development

Personnel Cost and Allocation

4. Compensation
5. Benefits
6. Staffing Patterns and Scheduling

Center Operations

7. Facilities Management
8. Risk Management
9. Internal Communications

Child Assessment

10. Screening and Identification of Special Needs
11. Assessment in Support of Learning

Fiscal Management

12. Budget Planning
13. Accounting Practices

Program Planning and Evaluation

14. Program Evaluation
15. Strategic Planning

Family Partnerships

16. Family Communications
17. Family Support and Involvement

Marketing and Public Relations

18. External Communications
19. Community Outreach

Technology

20. Technological Resources
21. Use of Technology

Staff Qualifications

22. Administrator
23. Lead Teacher
24. Teacher
25. Apprentice Teacher/Aide

Human Resources Development

1. Staff Orientation

Notes	Questions
Documents needed: orientation procedures, orientation checklist, orientation assessment tool, employee handbook, and personnel policies.	What happens when a new employee is hired? • What written materials about the center and/or program does the new employee receive? • Is there an introductory/probationary period with feedback provided by a supervisor?
* Written orientation procedures must describe the timeline, activities, and the personnel involved in the orientation process; identify the specific employment forms required; and specify written policies and procedures to be provided to new staff.	Do teaching staff observe the children and routines in their assigned classrooms/groups before assuming their responsibilities?
** A review is evidenced by written orientation procedures that are dated or minutes of a board or staff meeting indicating when a review occurred.	Are there written orientation procedures? • What do they include? • Are they reviewed? • How often?
*** A system requires tangible, concrete evidence (e.g., a checklist), involvement of multiple individuals, and a defined process of accountability.	Does the center provide a formal or informal orientation for new staff? • Is orientation provided consistently for all new staff? • Is there a systematic process for ensuring adequate orientation? • Is the orientation process evaluated?

Human Resources Development

1. Staff Orientation

1	2	3	4	5	6	7
Inadequate		**Minimal**		**Good**		**Excellent**

___ 1.1 There is no orientation for new staff.

___ 3.1
D includes receipt of the job description, employee handbook, parent handbook, and personnel policies.

___ 5.1
D The orientation includes feedback from the supervisor during the introductory or probationary period.

___ 7.1
D The orientation for new teaching staff includes observation in the assigned classroom and meeting children and coworkers prior to assuming responsibilities.

___ 1.2 There are no written orientation procedures.

___ 3.2
D There are written orientation procedures.*

___ 5.2
D The written orientation procedures have been reviewed within the last 3 years.**

___ 7.2
D The written orientation procedures are reviewed annually.**

___ 1.3 Staff orientation is not consistently implemented.

___ 3.3 Staff orientation is consistently implemented.

___ 5.3
D There is a system to ensure that staff orientation is consistently implemented.***

___ 7.3
D An assessment of the orientation process is conducted at the conclusion of the introductory or probationary period.

Comments:

Circle the final score based on the scoring rules on page 5.

1 2 3 4 5 6 7

1. Staff Orientation

2. Supervision and Performance Appraisal

Notes	Questions
Documents needed: example of performance appraisals (both supervisor's and staff's self-appraisal), job descriptions, examples of written feedback.	How is staff performance evaluated at the center? • How often does performance appraisal occur? • Who participates? • Does the performance appraisal process include annual goal setting?
* Teaching staff includes: Lead Teachers, Teachers, and Apprentice Teachers/Aides.	What criteria are used to evaluate performance? • Are criteria trait-based or behavior-based? • Are criteria tied to the responsibilities detailed in the employee's job description?
** An observation of teaching staff is formal when it is planned for the exclusive purpose of assessing and improving teaching practices.	What kind of supervision is provided for teaching staff at the center? • Are teaching staff observed? How often? • Is oral or written feedback provided? How often? • Is there a systematic process for ensuring adequate supervision?
*** A system requires tangible, concrete evidence, involvement of multiple individuals, and a defined process of accountability. Evidence of a system may include: assigned mentors, use of a feedback form indicating areas of strength as well as areas in need of improvement, use of videotaped classroom practices for coaching purposes, use of reflections or journaling for use in supervision, or regularly scheduled individual meetings with a supervisor or mentor.	

2. Supervision and Performance Appraisal

1	2	3	4	5	6	7
Inadequate		**Minimal**		**Good**		**Excellent**

___ 1.1 Written annual performance appraisal is not conducted for teaching staff.*

___ 3.1 D Written annual performance appraisal is conducted by supervisor for teaching staff.*

___ 5.1 D Teaching staff participate in annual performance appraisal process (e.g., written self-appraisal in file along with supervisor's appraisal).*

___ 7.1 D Written performance appraisal includes goals and professional development targets for the next year.

___ 1.2 Criteria used for performance appraisal are mostly subjective and trait-based (e.g., teacher is warm, friendly, caring).

___ 3.2 D Criteria used for performance appraisal are mostly objective and behavior-based (e.g., teacher uses positive guidance techniques, asks children open-ended questions).

___ 5.2 D Performance appraisal criteria differ by role and are tied to the specific responsibilities detailed in each job description.

___ 7.2 D Performance appraisal includes multiple sources of evidence (e.g., artifacts, parent feedback, co-worker feedback).

___ 1.3 Teaching staff are not formally observed as part of the supervision and performance appraisal process.**

___ 3.3 Teaching staff are formally observed as part of the supervision and performance appraisal process.**

___ 5.3 At least three times a year, supervisors provide teaching staff with written or oral feedback based on observation of the teacher's performance.

___ 7.3 D A system is implemented to provide ongoing feedback and support to teaching staff.***

Comments:

Circle the final score based on the scoring rules on page 5.

1   2   3   4   5   6   7

2. Supervision and Performance Appraisal

3. Staff Development

Notes	Questions
Documents needed: personnel policies, employee handbook, individual and center-wide professional development plans, individual staff training logs, and dated minutes of staff meetings or memos describing publicly funded professional development options.	Is staff development provided for all teaching, support, and administrative staff? Describe.

Notes:

*   Staff development includes on-site training as well as off-site classes, conferences, or workshops.

**   **Teaching staff** includes: Lead Teachers, Teachers, and Apprentice Teachers/Aides.
Support staff includes: cook, bus driver, clerical, and maintenance staff.
Administrative staff includes: Administrator, assistant director, social worker, and coordinators for education, curriculum, or family support.

***   A system requires tangible, concrete evidence, involvement of multiple individuals, and a defined process of accountability.

Questions:

Is staff development provided for all teaching, support, and administrative staff? Describe.

Does the center have a policy requiring a minimum number of staff development hours each year?
- Do individual staff members choose how to meet this professional development requirement?

Are staff advised about publicly funded professional development opportunities?
- Is there a systematic process for communicating this information?

3. Staff Development

	1	2	3	4	5	6	7
	Inadequate		**Minimal**		**Good**		**Excellent**

___ 1.1 No provision is made for staff development.*

___ 3.1 D Staff development for all teaching staff is provided on-site or paid for off-site.*

___ 5.1 D Staff development is provided for all teaching, support, and administrative staff.**

___ 7.1 D Job-specific staff development is provided (e.g., administrators receive training on strategic planning).

___ 1.2 Teaching and administrative staff attend less than 15 clock hours of staff development each year.

___ 3.2 D All teaching and administrative staff attend 15 or more clock hours of staff development each year.

___ 5.2 D All teaching and administrative staff attend 20 or more clock hours of staff development each year.

___ 7.2 D An individualized model of staff development is utilized for the teaching and administrative staff (specific training needs are identified and a plan to meet those needs is developed).

___ 1.3 The on-site Administrator is unfamiliar with publicly funded professional development opportunities available to staff.

___ 3.3 The on-site Administrator is familiar with publicly funded professional development opportunities available to staff (e.g., T.E.A.C.H. scholarships) and knows whom to contact for additional information.

___ 5.3 D Information regarding publicly funded professional development opportunities is posted and/or communicated to staff on an ongoing basis.

___ 7.3 D A system exists to support the career development of staff (e.g., regularly scheduled time to meet with a supervisor or mentor to monitor progress towards career goals; T.E.A.C.H. scholarships are utilized).***

Comments:

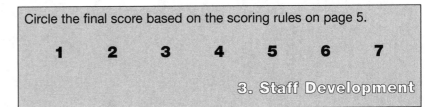

Circle the final score based on the scoring rules on page 5.

1   2   3   4   5   6   7

3. Staff Development

Personnel Cost and Allocation

4. Compensation

Notes	Questions
Documents needed: salary scale, compensation plan, and dated minutes or memos describing salary/wage increases.	Does the center have a written salary scale? • Who has access to the salary scale? • How often is it reviewed?
* Evidence of availability of salary scale to all staff is found in employee handbook, personnel policies, written orientation procedures, and/or orientation checklist.	What criteria is the salary scale based on? • Is it based on different roles? • Is it based on different levels of education and specialized training? • Is it based on experience?
** Salary scale must be dated within the past three years.	Does the staff receive an annual salary increase?
*** Education refers to the level of general education (e.g., high school diploma, associate degree, bachelor's degree). Specialized training refers to coursework in early childhood education or child development.	Does the staff receive merit increases in addition to annual salary increases?

Personnel Cost and Allocation

4. Compensation

1	2	3	4	5	6	7
Inadequate		**Minimal**		**Good**		**Excellent**

___ 1.1 A written salary scale is not available.

___ 3.1 D There is a written salary scale, and it is available to some center staff.

___ 5.1 D A written salary scale is available to all center staff.*

___ 7.1 D The written salary scale is reviewed at least every three years for internal and external equity.**

___ 1.2 A salary scale is based on role without regard to education and specialized training. ***

___ 3.2 D Salary scale is differentiated by role, education, and specialized training.***

___ 5.2 D Salary scale is differentiated by role, education, specialized training, and years of relevant experience.***

___ 7.2 D Staff with comparable education, specialized training, and experience are paid comparable wages for comparable work.***

___ 1.3 Staff did not receive a salary increase within the last two years.

___ 3.3 D Staff received a salary increase within the last two years.

___ 5.3 D Staff received an annual salary increase in each of the last three years.

___ 7.3 D The center has a compensation plan that provides for merit increases in addition to annual salary increases.

Comments:

Circle the final score based on the scoring rules on page 5.

| 1 | 2 | 3 | 4 | 5 | 6 | 7 |

4. Compensation

5. Benefits

Notes	Questions
Documents needed: personnel policies, employee handbook, and sample employee contract.	What health benefits are available to full-time staff? • What percentage of the employee's premium is paid by the organization?
* Full-time employment is defined as 35 or more hours per week of paid work unless the organization defines full-time employment differently as noted in the center's personnel policies or employee handbook.	What sick/personal day benefits are available to the staff? What paid vacation benefits are available to the staff? What retirement benefits are available to full-time staff?
** Part-time staff receive benefits proportionate to their hours of work.	What professional development or tuition reimbursement benefits are available to staff? • Is there a specific dollar amount available?

5. Benefits

	1	2	3	4	5	6	7
	Inadequate		**Minimal**		**Good**		**Excellent**

___ 1.1 All full-time staff do not have the option to purchase health insurance with the employer paying a portion of the cost.*

___ 3.1 D All full-time staff have the option to purchase health insurance with the employer paying a portion of the cost of the employee's coverage.*

___ 5.1 D All full-time staff have the option to purchase health insurance with the employer paying 50% or more of the cost of the employee's coverage.*

___ 7.1 D All full-time staff have the option to purchase health insurance with the employer paying 66% or more of the cost of the employee's coverage.*

___ 1.2 All staff do not receive at least 6 paid sick/personal days per year.**

___ 3.2 D All staff receive 6 or more paid sick/personal days per year.**

___ 5.2 D All staff receive 9 or more paid sick/personal days per year.**

___ 7.2 D All staff receive 12 or more paid sick/personal days per year.**

___ 1.3 All staff do not receive paid vacation time.**

___ 3.3 D All staff receive 5 or more paid vacation days during their first year of employment.**

___ 5.3 D All staff receive 10 or more paid vacation days per year during their second and third years of employment.**

___ 7.3 D All staff receive 15 or more paid vacation days per year after their third year of employment.**

___ 1.4 All full-time staff do not have the option of contributing to a retirement plan.*

___ 3.4 D All full-time staff (that meet the requirements set by the plan) have the option of contributing to a retirement plan.*

___ 5.4 D The employer matches 3% or more of the employee's salary contributed to a retirement plan.

___ 7.4 D The employer matches 5% or more of the employee's salary contributed to a retirement plan.

___ 1.5 No provision is made to reimburse tuition or other professional development expenses.

___ 3.5 D Some provision is made to reimburse tuition or other professional development expenses.

___ 5.5 D All teaching staff receive $100 or more per year for tuition or other professional development expenses.**

___ 7.5 D All teaching staff receive $200 or more per year for tuition or other professional development expenses.**

Comments:

Circle the final score based on the scoring rules on page 5.

1   2   3   4   5   6   7

5. Benefits

6. Staffing Patterns and Scheduling

Notes	Questions
Documents needed: staffing plan.	How often are children regrouped to maintain required ratios?
	• Are they regrouped at the beginning or end of the day?
* An unplanned absence occurs when staff are sick or take personal time. A planned absence occurs when staff take vacation time and/or released time for professional development.	• How is classroom coverage ensured when a member of the teaching staff is absent?
	Are members of the teaching staff given paid planning and preparation time?
** Paid planning and preparation time can occur during the children's naptime as long as it does not interfere with the adequate supervision of children.	• How often?
	• Who is included?
	Is a staff member ever alone with a child in the center?
	• In the classroom?
	How often does the Administrator spend time in the classroom to maintain required ratios?

6. Staffing Patterns and Scheduling

1	2	3	4	5	6	7
Inadequate		**Minimal**		**Good**		**Excellent**

___ 1.1 Children are regrouped to maintain required ratios six or more times per year.

___ 3.1 Children are regrouped to maintain required ratios less than six times per year.

___ 5.1 D The staffing plan provides classroom coverage so that children are not regrouped at the beginning or end of the day.

___ 7.1 D The staffing plan anticipates planned and unplanned absences of teaching staff by providing "staffing over ratio" or a "floating teacher."*

___ 1.2 There is no regularly scheduled paid planning or preparation time for teaching staff.**

___ 3.2 D There is regularly scheduled paid planning or preparation time for teaching staff.**

___ 5.2 D Paid planning time occurs at least every other week and includes all teaching staff working with the same group of children.

___ 7.2 D Teaching staff have the equivalent of at least one paid hour per day to prepare lessons and document children's learning and development.

___ 1.3 At times, a staff member is alone in the center with one or more children.

___ 3.3 D A staff member is never alone in the center with one or more children.

___ 5.3 D In each classroom there are two or more assigned teaching staff at all times children are present (exception allowed during the first and last hour of operation).

___ 7.3 D In each classroom there are two or more assigned teaching staff at all times children are present (including the first and last hour of operation).

___ 1.4 The Administrator spends time in a classroom to maintain required ratios more than once a week (N/A for programs with less than 50 children).

___ 3.4 The Administrator spends time in a classroom to maintain required ratios no more than once a week (N/A for programs with less than 50 children).

___ 5.4 The Administrator spends time in a classroom to maintain required ratios no more than once a month (N/A for programs with less than 50 children).

___ 7.4 The Administrator spends time in a classroom to maintain required ratios no more than four times per year (N/A for programs with less than 50 children).

Comments:

Circle the final score based on the scoring rules on page 5.

1   2   3   4   5   6   7

6. Staffing Patterns and Scheduling

7. Facilities Management

Notes	Questions

Documents needed: maintenance checklists, written safety procedures, and maintenance contracts.

* Safe and healthy appearance means that the overall impression is that the facility (classrooms, entry, hallways, kitchen, bathrooms), equipment (e.g., stove, refrigerator, video cart), and outdoor play environment (permanent equipment, landscaping, fencing, storage areas) are clean and well-maintained.

** Examples of routine maintenance might include: contracts for cleaning services and contracts for maintenance of the furnace, cooling system, playground equipment, fire extinguishers, and emergency alarm system.

*** A system of routine maintenance requires tangible, concrete evidence (e.g., a posted record of daily sanitation procedures implemented in bathrooms or a posted record of daily safety checks implemented in classrooms with sign-off by whom and when completed), involvement of multiple individuals, and a defined process of accountability.

**** Space that meets the needs of staff includes a separate adult restroom, a storage area for personal belongings, and adult-sized furniture.

What are standard operating procedures for routine maintenance?
• Is there a system in place to ensure compliance?

How does the space meet the needs of staff?

Is there office space on-site for program administration?
• How is the space equipped?

Center Operations

7. Facilities Management

1	2	3	4	5	6	7
Inadequate		**Minimal**		**Good**		**Excellent**

___ 1.1
O The facility and/or outdoor play environment appear unsafe or unhealthy.*

___ 3.1
O The facility and outdoor play environment appear safe and healthy.*

___ 5.1
D There is evidence of routine maintenance.**

___ 7.1
D There is a system of routine maintenance.***

___ 1.2
O Space is not provided for meeting the needs of staff.****

___ 3.2
O Space is provided for meeting the needs of staff.****

___ 5.2
O Space with adult-sized furniture is provided for staff use during breaks, meetings, conferences, and preparation time (dual use of space is allowed).

___ 7.2
O A separate staff lounge and a professional library are provided.

___ 1.3
O Office space for program administration is not available on-site.

___ 3.3
O Office space for program administration is available on-site.

___ 5.3
O Office space for program administration is equipped with file storage, a computer and printer, Internet access, copier, fax machine, and telephone with voice mail or answering machine.

___ 7.3
O Separate office space for the Administrator is available on-site allowing for private conversations and meetings.

Comments:

Circle the final score based on the scoring rules on page 5.

1   2   3   4   5   6   7

7. Facilities Management

8. Risk Management

Notes	Questions
Documents needed: risk management plan, children's allergies posted in classrooms, child intake form asking about chronic medical conditions, record of emergency drills, and annual training plan.	Does the center have a written risk management plan? • Where is it located? • What does the risk management plan include? • How often is the plan reviewed?
* The center's risk management plan must include: clear procedures to follow in the event of an emergency (e.g., fire, severe storm, power outage, sewer backup, intruder, accident, or illness); guidelines to reduce the risk of child abuse or neglect allegations; and procedures to maintain the safety of people, facilities, equipment, and materials.	How is information about children's allergies and chronic medical conditions documented? • How is the information communicated to staff? • How is the information communicated to substitutes?
** Examples might include: dated risk management plan, dated memo describing review of risk management plan, or minutes from a staff meeting where the risk management plan was reviewed.	How often are emergency drills implemented? • How are the drills evaluated? • Is there a system to ensure compliance?
*** A system requires tangible, concrete evidence (e.g., chart with assigned roles, written procedures, and checklists), involvement of multiple individuals, and a defined process of accountability.	Are employees trained in CPR and First Aid? • How many staff members are required to have the training?

8. Risk Management

1	2	3	4	5	6	7
Inadequate		**Minimal**		**Good**		**Excellent**

___ 1.1 No written risk management plan is available.

___ 3.1 D A written risk management plan is available.*

___ 5.1 A written risk management plan is available in each classroom.*

___ 7.1 D There is evidence that the written risk management plan is reviewed annually.**

___ 1.2 Information on individual children's allergies is not posted in the classroom, nor is information about children's chronic medical conditions kept in the office files.

___ 3.2 D Information on individual children's allergies is posted in the classroom **and** information about children's chronic medical conditions is kept in the office files.

___ 5.2 Information about individual children's chronic medical conditions is kept in the children's classrooms as well as in the office files.

___ 7.2 D A system is in place to ensure that necessary medical information is available to all teaching staff (including substitute teachers).***

___ 1.3 During the past year, fire drills were not practiced once a month.

___ 3.3 D During the past year, fire drills were practiced once a month **and** severe storm drills were practiced twice a year.

___ 5.3 The fire and severe storm drill records include an evaluation of the drills and improvements needed.

___ 7.3 D A system is in place to ensure that emergency drills occur as planned.***

___ 1.4 Center does not have at least one staff person trained in CPR and First Aid on-site during all hours of operation.

___ 3.4 Center has at least one staff person trained in CPR and First Aid on-site during all hours of operation.

___ 5.4 Center has at least one staff person in each classroom trained in CPR and First Aid.

___ 7.4 D Center provides annual training on CPR and First Aid procedures for all staff.

Comments:

Circle the final score based on the scoring rules on page 5.

1   2   3   4   5   6   7

8. Risk Management

9. Internal Communications

Notes	**Questions**
Documents needed: samples of center-wide staff meeting agendas and minutes, conflict resolution training materials, conflict resolution policy and procedures, and examples of different modes of communication.	What methods are used at the center to communicate information to staff?
	Are there regularly scheduled staff meetings at the center?
	• How often do staff meetings occur?
	• Who attends staff meetings?
* Examples of different modes of communication include: verbal communication, in-house newsletters, internal memos, e-mail, staff bulletin board, voicemail, message book, or routing slips.	Are staff members involved in planning and/or facilitating staff meetings?
	• Describe their level of involvement.
	Are minutes of staff meetings maintained?
	• How are minutes used?
	Does the center have a written policy regarding conflict resolution?
	• Does the center have written procedures for staff to follow to resolve disputes?

9. Internal Communications

1	2	3	4	5	6	7
Inadequate		**Minimal**		**Good**		**Excellent**

___ 1.1 Information is communicated only verbally.

___ 3.1 D Information is communicated in more than one way.*

___ 5.1 D Information is communicated in three or more ways.*

___ 7.1 D Information is communicated in five or more ways.*

___ 1.2 There are no regularly scheduled, center-wide staff meetings.

___ 3.2 D There are regularly scheduled, center-wide staff meetings that occur at least two times a year.

___ 5.2 D There are regularly scheduled staff meetings that occur at least once a month (may include team or center-wide meetings).

___ 7.2 D There are regularly scheduled staff meetings that occur at least twice a month (may include team or center-wide meetings).

___ 1.3 Staff are not involved in planning center-wide staff meetings.

___ 3.3 Staff are involved in planning center-wide staff meetings.

___ 5.3 D Staff occasionally lead the discussion of agenda items during center-wide staff meetings.

___ 7.3 D Staff consistently plan and facilitate discussion of agenda items during center-wide staff meetings.

___ 1.4 There are no records kept of topics discussed and decisions made at staff meetings.

___ 3.4 D Minutes are kept of staff meetings documenting topics discussed and decisions made.

___ 5.4 D Minutes reflect an action plan (e.g., activities planned, timelines, check points, and who will be accountable).

___ 7.4 D Minutes are distributed in advance of staff meetings and action steps are revisited at subsequent meetings.

___ 1.5 There is no written policy regarding the handling of staff disputes.

___ 3.5 D There is a written policy regarding the handling of staff disputes.

___ 5.5 D Staff are provided with professional resources and/or training in conflict resolution.

___ 7.5 D There are written procedures to guide staff efforts at conflict resolution.

Comments:

Circle the final score based on the scoring rules on page 5.

1   2   3   4   5   6   7

9. Internal Communications

Child Assessment

10. Screening and Identification of Special Needs

Notes	Questions

Documents needed: developmental screening instrument.
 	
*   Screening refers to the first step in a two-step process of identification of disabilities such as vision or hearing impairment, physical disabilities, speech and language impairment, emotional disturbance, mental retardation, and specific learning disabilities and developmental delays. The second step is further evaluation.
 	
**   Examples of valid and reliable screening tools include Ages and Stages, the Brigance, and the Early Screening Inventory Preschool (ESI-P).
 	
***   Safeguards include: screenings are conducted and interpreted by trained professionals, multiple sources of evidence are used (parent and staff input from home and center observations), screening measures are never the sole source used to identify children for special education, and children are assessed in their primary language.
 	
****   A special plan refers to adaptations made by the teaching staff regarding classroom routines, activities, or daily schedule.
 	
*****   A system requires tangible, concrete evidence (e.g., chart with assigned roles, written procedures, and checklists), involvement of multiple individuals, and a defined process of accountability.
	Are all children in the center, birth to age 5, screened for the purpose of identifying special needs?
	   • What screening tool is used?
	   • Does the screening tool have established reliability and validity?
	   • Are there safeguards to protect against misidentification of children?
	
	What is the role of parents before and after the screening and identification of children with special needs?
	
	Does the program make referrals for children identified with special needs?
	   • Is there a system to collaborate with specialists working with identified children?

Child Assessment

10. Screening and Identification of Special Needs

1	2	3	4	5	6	7
Inadequate		Minimal		Good		Excellent

___ 1.1 Children are not screened for the purpose of identifying special needs.*

___ 3.1 All children, birth to age 5, are screened for the purpose of identifying special needs.*

___ 5.1 All children, birth to age 5, D are screened using a valid and reliable screening tool.**

___ 7.1 To protect against misidentification, a minimum of two safeguards are built into the identification process.***

___ 1.2 Parental consent is not obtained prior to screening (N/A is allowed).

___ 3.2 Parental consent is obtained prior to screening (N/A is allowed).

___ 5.2 Parents are informed of the results of screening if a possible developmental delay or disability is identified.

___ 7.2 Parents are informed about any special plans made for their children based on screening; such plans are documented in the child's file.****

___ 5.3 Children identified in the screening process are referred to specialists (e.g., physician or child study team) for further evaluation.

___ 7.3 A system is in place to support D collaboration with specialists working with identified children.*****

Comments:

Circle the final score based on the scoring rules on page 5.

1	2	3	4	5	6	7

10. Screening and Identification of Special Needs

11. Assessment in Support of Learning

Notes	Questions
Documents needed: child assessment form, developmental checklist, lesson plans, written record of use of aggregated assessment data for evaluation and planning, and an example of a child's portfolio.	How do teaching staff assess children's learning and development? • Do teaching staff conduct formal observations of children? • Do teaching staff use assessment tools with established reliability and validity? • Do teaching staff maintain a portfolio of individual children's work?
* Reliable and valid assessments include research-based checklists (e.g., High/Scope COR, Work Sampling System, Creative Curriculum).	How is the curriculum planned at the center? • Is the curriculum based on professional standards? • Are children's individual outcomes considered? • Are data regarding children's assessments aggregated and used for curriculum planning?
** Standards refer to published professional standards (e.g., NAEYC, NSACCA, Head Start Outcomes Framework) or individual state learning standards.	

11. Assessment in Support of Learning

	1	2	3	4	5	6	7
	Inadequate		**Minimal**		**Good**		**Excellent**

___ 1.1 No assessment is in place for observing children and assessing their learning and development.

___ 3.1 Assessment includes
D teaching staff making judgments using assessment checklists (may be teacher-made).

___ 5.1 Assessment includes
D teaching staff making judgments using assessment checklists that are reliable and valid.*

___ 7.1 Assessment includes
D teaching staff making judgments using reliable and valid checklists as well as other measures (e.g., portfolios of children's work, teacher's observational notes).*

___ 1.2 Standards are not considered in curriculum planning.**

___ 3.2 Standards are considered in
D curriculum planning.**

___ 5.2 Individual assessment results
D regarding child outcomes are utilized in curriculum planning.

___ 7.2 Aggregated assessment
D results regarding child outcomes are utilized in long-range curriculum planning and/or in program evaluation.

Adapted from *Best Practices in Early Childhood Assessment* and used with permission of Judy Harris Helm, Best Practices, Inc.

Comments:

Circle the final score based on the scoring rules on page 5.

1   2   3   4   5   6   7

11. Assessment in Support of Learning

Fiscal Management

12. Budget Planning

Notes	Questions
Documents needed: current operating budget, projected budget, written policy and procedures about collecting tuition and fees, and written program goals.	How is the on-site Administrator involved in program budget planning?

Does the budget reflect the program's written goals?

Does the center have an operating budget for the current fiscal year?
    • Does the center have a projected budget for the coming year?

Are payroll, taxes, and insurance expenses paid by the due date?
    • Describe procedures to ensure adequate cash flow. |

*   Expenditures need to reflect the written goals; revenues need to match expenditures.

**   Adequate cash-flow practices include the prompt deposit of income, methods for informing parents about money owed, and clear policies and procedures regarding the collection of delinquent tuition and fees.

Fiscal Management

12. Budget Planning

	1	2	3	4	5	6	7
	Inadequate		**Minimal**		**Good**		**Excellent**

___ 1.1 The on-site Administrator is not involved in developing the program budget.

___ 3.1 The on-site Administrator is involved in developing the program budget.

___ 5.1 D Program needs assessment and goal setting are an integral part of the annual budget-planning process.

___ 7.1 D The annual budget includes sufficient resources to achieve the program's written goals.*

___ 1.2 A current year operating budget, including revenue and expenses, is not available.

___ 3.2 D A current year operating budget, including revenue and expenses, is available.

___ 5.2 D The operating budget has line-item breakdowns to permit effective monitoring of revenue and expenses.

___ 7.2 D A projected operating budget for the next fiscal year is available by the beginning of the fourth quarter of the current fiscal year.

___ 1.3 There are regular instances when payroll, insurance, or taxes are not paid on time.

___ 3.3 All payroll, insurance, and taxes are paid on time.

___ 5.3 D The budget reflects deferred maintenance and capital improvements, as well as equipment replacement expenses (e.g., computers).

___ 7.3 D Quarterly and annual cash-flow projections and other accepted practices provide for adequate cash flow.**

Comments:

Circle the final score based on the scoring rules on page 5.

1   2   3   4   5   6   7

12. Budget Planning

13. Accounting Practices

Notes	Questions
Documents needed: quarterly financial statements, most recent audit, policy regarding separation of financial duties, and examples of cancelled checks with multiple signatures.	How often are income and expense statements prepared?
	Does the on-site Administrator have access to income and expense statements?
* A system requires tangible, concrete evidence, involvement of multiple individuals, and a defined process of accountability.	• Provide an example of how this information is used to make program decisions.
** The elements of a system of checks and balances might include: two or more signatures required on checks, the separation of restricted funds (grants) and major capital funds from general operating funds, and the separation of duties (e.g., the same person does not receive cash and authorize cash disbursements).	Does the center have a system of checks and balances? • Describe the elements of this system.

*** Independent review means that the reviewer is not an employee of the organization. A board member or parent can conduct an independent review.	Is there an independent review of accounting records?
	   • By whom?
	   • How often?

13. Accounting Practices

1	2	3	4	5	6	7
Inadequate		**Minimal**		**Good**		**Excellent**

___ 1.1 A system does not exist to generate quarterly income and expense statements.*

___ 3.1 D A system exists to generate quarterly income and expense statements. *

___ 5.1 D The on-site Administrator has access to or generates quarterly income and expense statements.

___ 7.1 The on-site Administrator uses quarterly income and expense statements to monitor the center's fiscal status and make programmatic decisions.

___ 1.2 There is no accounting system of checks and balances.**

___ 3.2 D There is one element of a checks-and-balances system.**

___ 5.2 D There are two elements of a checks-and-balances system.**

___ 7.2 D There are three elements of a checks-and-balances system.**

___ 1.3 There is no independent review of the accounting records (reconciliation of the bank statements to the general ledger).***

___ 3.3 There is an independent review of the accounting records (reconciliation of bank statements to the general ledger).***

___ 5.3 There is a quarterly review of the accounting records by an independent third party who has accounting or bookkeeping expertise.***

___ 7.3 D An outside audit is conducted annually by a certified public accountant.

Comments:

Circle the final score based on the scoring rules on page 5.

1   2   3   4   5   6   7

13. Accounting Practices

14. Program Evaluation

Notes	Questions
Documents needed: samples of parent and staff questionnaires, organizational climate assessment, evidence of solicitied feedback, accreditation documents, Head Start Performance Standards self assessment, and written program-improvement plans.	Are the staff involved in evaluating the program? • Do they use an assessment tool? If yes, how often? • What other mechanisms are used to elicit feedback from the staff about the quality of the program?
* Examples include: a suggestion box, message book, informal questionnaire, organizational climate assessment, evidence of availability of director to meet informally with parents or staff, and agenda items or other evidence of solicited feedback at staff or parent meetings.	Are parents involved in evaluating the program? • Do they use an assessment tool? If yes, how often? • What other mechanisms are used to elicit feedback from the parents on the quality of the program? How is the information gathered from staff and parent evaluations used? • Provide some specific examples.

Program Planning and Evaluation

14. Program Evaluation

	1	2	3	4	5	6	7
	Inadequate		**Minimal**		**Good**		**Excellent**

___ 1.1 No assessment tool is used by staff to evaluate the program.

___ 3.1 D An assessment tool is used occasionally (every 2–3 years) by staff to evaluate the program.

___ 5.1 D An assessment tool is used annually by staff to evaluate the program.

___ 7.1 D The center has two or more additional ways to obtain informal feedback about program quality from staff.*

___ 1.2 No assessment tool is used by parents to evaluate the program.

___ 3.2 D An assessment tool is used occasionally (every 2–3 years) by parents to evaluate the program.

___ 5.2 D An assessment tool is used annually by parents to evaluate the program.

___ 7.2 D The center has two or more additional ways to obtain informal feedback about program quality from parents.*

___ 1.3 Program decision making is not influenced by parent and staff evaluations of the program.

___ 3.3 Program decisions are influenced by parent and staff evaluations of the program.

___ 5.3 D Data from parent and staff evaluations are used to develop a written plan for program improvement.

___ 7.3 D The center's evaluation system includes a feedback loop to staff and parents demonstrating the influence of their input.

Comments:

Circle the final score based on the scoring rules on page 5.

1   2   3   4   5   6   7

14. Program Evaluation

15. Strategic Planning

Notes	Questions
Documents needed: mission or vision statement, business plan or strategic plan, and dated minutes or memos indicating staff and/or governing board review.	Does the center have a written mission or vision statement? • How often is the mission or vision statement reviewed? • Who is involved in the review process?
* The business plan or strategic plan is a document that must include: a needs assessment, plan for services, short- and long-term goals, and strategies to achieve goals (e.g., marketing, enrollment, salary, or financial plans).	Does the center have a written business plan or strategic plan? • How often is the business or strategic plan reviewed? • Who is involved in the review process?

15. Strategic Planning

	1		2		3		4		5		6		7	
	Inadequate				**Minimal**				**Good**				**Excellent**	

___ 1.1 The center does not have a written mission or vision statement.

___ 3.1
D The center has a written mission or vision statement.

___ 5.1
D The staff and governing board (if a nonprofit organization) were involved in developing a written mission or vision statement.

___ 7.1
D The center's mission or vision statement is reviewed at least every five years by staff and governing board (if a nonprofit organization).

___ 1.2 The center does not have a written business plan or strategic plan.

___ 3.2
D The center has a written business plan or strategic plan.*

___ 5.2
D Staff and governing board (if a nonprofit organization) were involved in developing a written business plan or strategic plan.*

___ 7.2
D The center's written business plan or strategic plan is reviewed annually by staff and governing board (if a nonprofit organization) to evaluate the center's progress in achieving goals.*

Comments:

Circle the final score based on the scoring rules on page 5.

1   2   3   4   5   6   7

15. Strategic Planning

Family Partnerships

16. Family Communications

Notes	Questions
Documents needed: intake form, parent handbook, family orientation procedures, newsletter, website information, sample of items from parent bulletin board, message log, and agenda/minutes of parent meetings.	How are new families oriented to the center? Do staff members create and maintain open communication with families about their values, beliefs, and culture? • How is this achieved?

* Orientation procedures must include: providing parents with written information about center operations, schedule, fees, calendar, health requirements, and discipline policy. The orientation procedures must also include asking families for information about the child's development, strengths, likes, and dislikes.	What are the various ways the teaching staff communicate with families?
	
	Do teaching staff hold formal conferences with families?
	   • How often are conferences held?
	   • Are conferences held at times that are convenient for families?

** Enhanced orientation procedures must include: a guided tour of the center, an introduction to the teaching staff, an opportunity to ask questions of the Administrator, and information about family programming and family-friendly supports.	Does the center have a system to ensure daily communication between teaching staff and families? Describe.
*** A system requires tangible, concrete evidence (e.g., written policy and procedures; family orientation checklist; written, two-way communication logs). It also involves multiple participants and a defined process of accountability.	
**** Modes of communication include: informal conversation, periodic family meetings, newsletters, bulletin boards, notes that go home with children, mailed letters, e-mail, phone calls, and website.	

Family Partnerships

16. Family Communications

	1	2	3	4	5	6	7
	Inadequate		**Minimal**		**Good**		**Excellent**

___ 1.1 The center does not have an orientation procedure for new families.

___ 1.2 The staff do not ask families about their values, beliefs, and cultural and childrearing practices.

___ 1.3 The center does not communicate with families in their primary language or utilize resources as needed to communicate with families.

___ 1.4 The center does not provide for formal conferencing to discuss children's learning and development.

___ 3.1 The center has an orientation
D procedure for new families.*

___ 3.2 The staff ask families about
D their values, beliefs, and cultural and childrearing practices during the intake process.

___ 3.3 The center communicates
D with families in their primary language or utilizes resources as needed to communicate with families.

___ 3.4 The center provides for one
D formal conference per year at times that are convenient to working families.

___ 5.1 The center has enhanced
D family orientation procedures.**

___ 5.2 The family's perspective about
D childrearing and cultural practices is solicited during parent meetings or conferences to create or maintain open communication.

___ 5.3 The center regularly
D communicates with families by using five or more modes of communication.****

___ 5.4 The center provides for two
D formal conferences per year at times that are convenient for working families.

___ 7.1 The center has a system
D to check in with new families after a few weeks.***

___ 7.2 The center implements
D procedures to achieve consistency between home and center when possible (e.g., nap, menu, toileting).

___ 7.3 The center regularly
D communicates with families by using seven or more modes of communication.****

___ 7.4 A system exists to provide
D families with the opportunity for daily communication with teaching staff.***

Comments:

Circle the final score based on the scoring rules on page 5.

1	2	3	4	5	6	7

16. Family Communications

17. Family Support and Involvement

Notes	Questions

Documents needed: parent handbook and letters to families inviting them to participate in center events or classroom activities; dated minutes, logs, or newsletters detailing family participation in center events and classroom activities.

* Family support refers to the variety of ways that a center is responsive to family needs. Examples of family-friendly supports include:

- Children's book or toy lending library
- Family resource library
- Child care for sick or mildly ill children
- Extended care during evenings or weekends
- Information and referral to supportive services regarding family issues
- Convenience services (take-home meals, haircuts, photographs, or dry cleaning)
- Adult classes (literacy, computer, job training)
- Home visits
- Family meetings, seminars, or support groups
- Social functions for families and staff
- Child care during parent conferences or meetings
- Provision for food or clothing donations
- Transportation to and from the center
- Tuition scholarships

What are the various ways the staff support families who are enrolled in the program?

Are parents/guardians encouraged to visit the classroom?
- Are they allowed to visit at any time or only at specific times?
- Are members of the extended family allowed to visit in the classroom?

Are family members involved in center activities?
- Do they participate in parenting meetings and special events?
- Do they participate in routine classroom activities?
- Do they serve on the center's advisory or governing board?

17. Family Support and Involvement

1	2	3	4	5	6	7
Inadequate		**Minimal**		**Good**		**Excellent**

___ 1.1 The center offers no family supports.*

___ 1.2 Parents/guardians are not invited to visit in the classroom.

___ 1.3 There is no plan for involving families in the activities of the center.

___ 3.1 D The center offers at least three family supports.*

___ 3.2 D Parents/guardians are invited to visit in the classroom.

___ 3.3 D Families participate in parent meetings, special events, parties, and fieldtrips.

___ 5.1 D The center offers at least five family supports.*

___ 5.2 D Extended family members (grandparents, aunts, uncles) are welcome to visit in the classroom.

___ 5.3 D Families participate in routine classroom activities (e.g., reading books, assisting with story dictations, and helping with art projects).

___ 7.1 D The center offers at least seven family supports.*

___ 7.2 D Family members are invited to visit in the classroom at any time.

___ 7.3 D Family members serve on the center's advisory or governing board.

Comments:

Circle the final score based on the scoring rules on page 5.

1   2   3   4   5   6   7

17. Family Support and Involvement

Marketing and Public Relations

18. External Communications

Notes	Questions

Documents needed: public relations tools, dated minutes of board and/or staff meetings at which the public relations tools were reviewed, and dated log of enrollment inquiries and responses.

*   Public relations tools include: stationery, brochure, logo, business cards, signage, newsletter, website, advertising copy, phonebook advertisement, and promotional items (e.g., clothing, mugs).

**   "Projects a professional image" means the center uses a consistent logo and the promotional materials distributed are neat and grammatically correct.

***   As evidenced by dated minutes of board and/or staff meetings at which the public relations tools were reviewed.

What are the various public relations tools utilized by the center?
- Do the public relations tools display a consistent logo?
- Are the public relations tools reviewed?
- How often are they reviewed?

What happens when a prospective parent calls to inquire about the program?
- How quickly is follow-up information sent or communicated?
- Are records kept of inquiries?
- How are staff members trained to respond to inquiries?

Marketing and Public Relations

18. External Communications

1	2	3	4	5	6	7
Inadequate		**Minimal**		**Good**		**Excellent**

___ 1.1
D
The center utilizes fewer than three public relations tools.*

___ 3.1
D
The center utilizes three or more public relations tools.*

___ 5.1
D
The center utilizes five or more public relations tools.*

___ 7.1
D
The center utilizes seven or more public relations tools.*

___ 1.2
Public relations materials do not project a professional image.**

___ 3.2
D
Public relations materials project a professional image.**

___ 5.2
D
Public relations materials are reviewed to assure that information and photos are not outdated.***

___ 7.2
D
There is a systematic review by multiple stakeholders (e.g., parents, staff, board) of the public relations tools at least every three years.***

___ 1.3
Information about the center is not sent out nor are follow-up calls made in response to inquiries within 48 hours.

___ 3.3
Information about the center is sent out and/or follow-up calls are made in response to inquiries within 48 hours.

___ 5.3
D
Records are kept of all prospective parents who inquire about the center and follow-up action taken (e.g., call made, letter sent).

___ 7.3
D
Center has a written guide to train administrative and teaching staff in providing information to prospective parents who call or visit.

Comments:

Circle the final score based on the scoring rules on page 5.

1   2   3   4   5   6   7

18. External Communications

19. Community Outreach

Notes	Questions
Documents needed: memos, letters, and newsletters showing involvement with neighbors, the local community, and the early childhood professional community.	How are the Administrator or other members of the staff involved in local community organizations?
	What do the Administrator and the staff do to promote positive relations with the immediate neighborhood or local community?
* Examples of organizations in the local community include: Rotary, Chamber of Commerce, local business roundtable, local United Way, or community development agencies.	• Describe some of the strategies used to promote positive relationships.
** Involvement in the early childhood professional community can be demonstrated by membership in a directors' network, membership in the national or local AEYC or other early childhood organizations, or collaborating with the local elementary school to ensure smooth transitions.	Are the Administrator or other staff members involved in the early childhood professional community? • Describe the level of involvement.
*** Active role means that the Administrator or staff attend meetings regularly and serve on one or more committees of early childhood professional organizations.	
**** Leadership role means that the Administrator or staff chair a committee, serve on a board, or hold office in an early childhood organization.	

19. Community Outreach

	1	2	3	4	5	6	7
	Inadequate		**Minimal**		**Good**		**Excellent**

___ 1.1 The Administrator or staff do not attend events sponsored by organizations in the local community.*

___ 3.1 The Administrator and/or staff attend one or more events per year sponsored by organizations in the local community.*

___ 5.1 D The Administrator and/or staff are members of at least one organization in the local community.*

___ 7.1 D The Administrator and/or staff play a leadership role in a local community organization or actively collaborate with other local organizations.*

___ 1.2 The Administrator or staff appear indifferent to the center's impact on the immediate neighborhood or local community.

___ 3.2 The Administrator and/or staff show concern about being good neighbors (e.g., post reminders to parents and visitors about parking restrictions, maintain clean sidewalks).

___ 5.2 D The Administrator and/or staff seek opportunities to build good relations within the immediate neighborhood or local community (e.g., inviting neighbors to open houses, notifying them of special events, sending newsletters, using neighborhood resources for special projects).

___ 7.2 D There is evidence of support from the immediate neighborhood or local community (e.g., financial support, in-kind donated services, tangible gifts, discounted services, letters of support).

___ 1.3 The Administrator or staff have no involvement in the early childhood professional community.**

___ 3.3 D The Administrator and/or staff have some involvement in the early childhood professional community.**

___ 5.3 D The Administrator and/or staff play an active role in the early childhood professional community.***

___ 7.3 D The Administrator and/or staff played a leadership role in the early childhood professional community during the past three years.****

Comments:

Circle the final score based on the scoring rules on page 5.

1   2   3   4   5   6   7

19. Community Outreach

20. Technological Resources

Notes	Questions
Documents needed: technology polices and technology maintenance checklist.	Does the center have a computer and printer for administrative purposes?
	• Is it in working condition?
* A functional computer must be able to effectively run software that includes an operating system and an integrated office suite with programs for word processing, spreadsheet, database, and presentation graphics.	Does the center have computers and printers available for teaching staff to use?
	Does the center have a system to maintain, repair, and update computers and software? Describe.
** A system requires tangible, concrete evidence (e.g., technology policies, maintenance checklist), the involvement of multiple participants, and a defined process of accountability.	Does the center have Internet access?
	• Who has Internet access?

Technology

20. Technological Resources

1	2	3	4	5	6	7
Inadequate		**Minimal**		**Good**		**Excellent**

___ 1.1 The center does not have a functional computer and printer.*

___ 3.1 The center has a functional
O   computer and printer for administrative use.*

___ 5.1 The center has multiple
O   computers and printers that are available to teaching staff as well as administrative staff.

___ 7.1 The center has a system for
D   maintaining, updating, and replacing computers and software.**

___ 1.2 The center does not have Internet access.

___ 3.2 The center has Internet access
O   for administrative use.

___ 5.2 The center has Internet access
O   for teaching staff.

___ 7.2 The center has Internet access
O   available to teaching staff during staff planning and preparation time.

___ 5.3 The center has Internet access
O   for school-age children (N/A is allowed).

___ 7.3 The center has Internet access
O   in each school-age classroom (N/A is allowed).

Comments:

Circle the final score based on the scoring rules on page 5.

1   2   3   4   5   6   7

20. Technological Resources

21. Use of Technology

Notes	Questions
Documents needed: examples of word processing, spreadsheet, and database applications used by administrative and teaching staff.	Do administrative staff utilize word processing applications? • For what purposes?
	Do administrative staff utilize spreadsheet and database applications? • For what purposes?
* Applications using word processing software (e.g., Word, WordPerfect, WordPro) include: memos, letters, menus, proposals, reports, calendars, schedules, newsletters, brochures, mailing labels, and documentation of children's learning and development.	How do members of the teaching staff use technology in their work with children and families?
** Applications using spreadsheet and database software (e.g., Excel, Access, Lotus) include: general ledger, purchasing, accounts payable, accounts receivable, billing, payroll, general budget planning, cash flow forecasting, enrollment, database, employee benefits, medical records, and inventory monitoring.	
*** Examples of technology include: the use of tape recorders, cameras, camcorders, scanners, as well as computers.	

21. Use of Technology

1	2	3	4	5	6	7
Inadequate		**Minimal**		**Good**		**Excellent**

___ 1.1 Administrative staff do not use any word processing applications.*

___ 3.1 D Administrative staff use three or more word processing applications.*

___ 5.1 D Administrative staff use five or more word processing applications.*

___ 7.1 D Administrative staff use seven or more word processing applications.*

___ 1.2 Administrative staff do not use any spreadsheet or database applications.**

___ 3.2 D Administrative staff use three or more spreadsheet or database applications.**

___ 5.2 D Administrative staff use five or more spreadsheet or database applications.**

___ 7.2 D Administrative staff use seven or more spreadsheet or database applications.**

___ 1.3 Teaching staff do not use technology in their work with children and families.***

___ 3.3 D Teaching staff use technology in their work with children and families.***

___ 5.3 D Teaching staff regularly use technology in their work with children and families (e.g., documentation of children's learning, child assessment, calendars, parent letters).***

___ 7.3 Teaching staff regularly use the Internet (e.g., for curriculum planning, research, professional development, seeking resources for parents, or communicating with colleagues).

Comments:

Circle the final score based on the scoring rules on page 5.

1   2   3   4   5   6   7

21. Use of Technology

51

Staff Qualifications

22. Administrator

Notes	Data Collection Procedure
The **Administrator** is the person located on-site who has the primary responsibility for planning, implementing, and evaluating the early care and education program. Role titles for the administrator vary from program to program and may include director, manager, and principal.	Use the **Administrator Qualifications Worksheet** on page 62 to record information regarding the Administrator's general education, specialized training, experience, and professional contributions. This data can then be used to rate the indicators on the following page and generate an item score for Item 22.

The **Administrator** is the person located on-site who has the primary responsibility for planning, implementing, and evaluating the early care and education program. Role titles for the administrator vary from program to program and may include director, manager, and principal.

Depending on the type and size of the early childhood program, there may be several individuals who have administrative roles. **The rating for this item is based only on the background and qualifications of the individual designated as the on-site Administrator.** The *Program Administration Scale* does not include assessment of other administrative roles such as assistant director or education coordinator.

Documents needed: **Administrator Qualifications Worksheet**, Administrator's transcripts, professional portfolio (or other evidence of professional contributions), and evidence of management experience.

*   Management experience refers to the responsibility for program and budget planning, implementation, and evaluation. It can include experience as an assistant director or coordinator of a single program. A year of employment is defined as a minimum of 1,200 hours (a six-hour workday for an academic year).

**   Professional contributions are those activities that show commitment to the field of early childhood beyond daily center-based responsibilities. Professional contributions include: active service or leadership in an early childhood professional organization, serving as a resource to the media about early childhood issues (e.g., quoted in newspaper, guest on radio or cable show), presenting at professional conferences, providing training for another program, mentoring, advocacy, research, and writing/publishing.

Use the **Administrator Qualifications Worksheet** on page 62 to record information regarding the Administrator's general education, specialized training, experience, and professional contributions. This data can then be used to rate the indicators on the following page and generate an item score for Item 22.

Staff Qualifications

22. Administrator

	1		2		3		4		5		6		7	
	Inadequate				**Minimal**				**Good**				**Excellent**	

___ 1.1 The on-site Administrator has less than an associate degree or 60 sh of college credit.

___ 3.1 D The on-site Administrator has an associate degree or 60 or more sh of college credit.

___ 5.1 D The on-site Administrator has a baccalaureate degree.

___ 7.1 D The on-site Administrator has a master's or other advanced degree.

___ 1.2 The on-site Administrator has less than 18 sh of ECE/CD coursework.

___ 3.2 D The on-site Administrator has 21 or more sh of ECE/CD coursework.

___ 5.2 D The on-site Administrator has 24 or more sh of ECE/CD.

___ 7.2 D The on-site Administrator has 30 or more sh of ECE/CD coursework.

___ 1.3 The on-site Administrator has no college credit for management coursework.

___ 3.3 D The on-site Administrator has 9 or more sh of credit for management coursework.

___ 5.3 D The on-site Administrator has 15 or more sh of credit for management coursework.

___ 7.3 D The on-site Administrator has 21 or more sh of credit for management coursework.

___ 1.4 The on-site Administrator has less than one year of management experience.*

___ 3.4 D The on-site Administrator has one or more years of management experience.*

___ 5.4 D The on-site Administrator has three or more years of management experience.*

___ 7.4 D The on-site Administrator has more than five years of management experience.*

___ 5.5 D The on-site Administrator has made four or more professional contributions during the past three years.**

___ 7.5 D The on-site Administrator has made six or more professional contributions during the past three years.**

Comments:

Circle the final score based on the scoring rules on page 5.

1   2   3   4   5   6   7

22. Administrator

23. Lead Teacher

Notes	Data Collection Procedure

The **Lead Teacher** is the individual with the highest educational qualifications assigned to teach a group of children and who is responsible for daily lesson planning, parent conferences, child assessment, and curriculum planning. This individual may also supervise other members of the teaching team. In some settings, this person is called a head teacher, master teacher, or teacher.

Depending on the staffing pattern of the program, there may be several individuals working with a group of children who are responsible for their daily care and education. Regardless of the different role titles used by the center, **the rating of this item is based solely on the qualifications of the individual with the highest educational qualifications who is regularly assigned to teach a group/classroom of children**.

Documents needed: **Teaching Staff Qualifications Worksheet**, transcripts, and evidence of teaching experience.

*   A year of employment is defined as a minimum of 1,200 hours (a six-hour workday for an academic year).

---

1. Make copies of the **Teaching Staff Qualifications Worksheet** on page 63 so there is a separate worksheet for each group/classroom of children in the program. On the top of the worksheet write the name of the group/classroom.

2. In the designated space, write the initials of each member of the teaching staff regularly assigned to each group/classroom. This worksheet provides space for up to four members of the teaching staff for each group/classroom.

3. Provide the information regarding the education, specialized training, and experience of each member of the teaching staff regularly assigned to each group/classroom.

4. Determine which member of the teaching staff for each group/classroom has the highest educational qualifications. This individual will be designated as the Lead Teacher for purposes of completing Item 23.

5. Make additional copies of Item 23 (page 55) so that each individual designated as Lead Teacher (one for each group/classroom of children) has a separate Item 23 page. Complete the rating of Item 23 for each Lead Teacher and transfer this score to Column A on the **Summary of Teaching Staff Qualifications** on page 64.

6. Determine the average score for Item 23 by summing the individual Lead Teacher scores and dividing by the number of Lead Teachers (the same as the number of groups/classrooms). Record this Item 23 Average Score on the bottom of the **Summary of Teaching Staff Qualifications**.

23. Lead Teacher

	1	2	3	4	5	6	7
	Inadequate		**Minimal**		**Good**		**Excellent**

___ 1.1 Lead Teacher has less than an associate degree or 60 sh of college credit.

___ 3.1 Lead Teacher has an associate degree or has 60 sh of college credit and is enrolled in a BA degree program.
D

___ 5.1 Lead Teacher has a baccalaureate degree.
D

___ 7.1 Lead Teacher has a master's or other advanced degree.
D

___ 1.2 Lead Teacher has less than 12 sh of ECE/CD coursework.

___ 3.2 Lead Teacher has 21 or more sh of ECE/CD coursework.
D

___ 5.2 Lead Teacher has 30 or more sh of ECE/CD coursework.
D

___ 7.2 Lead Teacher has certification and is qualified to teach young children in a public school system.
D

___ 1.3 Lead Teacher has less than six months of experience teaching young children (birth to 8 years of age).*

___ 3.3 Lead Teacher has six or more months of experience teaching young children (birth to 8 years of age).*
D

___ 5.3 Lead Teacher has one or more years of experience teaching young children (birth to 8 years of age).*
D

___ 7.3 Lead Teacher has three or more years of experience teaching young children (birth to 8 years of age).*
D

Comments:

Circle the final score based on the scoring rules on page 5.

1   2   3   4   5   6   7

23. Lead Teacher

24. Teacher

Notes	Data Collection Procedure

A **Teacher** is a member of the teaching team who shares responsibility with the Lead Teacher for the care and education of an assigned group of children.

Depending on the staffing pattern of the program, there may be more than one person designated as Teacher for each group of children. It is also possible that a group of children will not have someone designated as Teacher on the teaching team.

Documents needed: **Teaching Staff Qualifications Worksheet**, transcripts, and evidence of teaching experience.

*   CDA = Child Development Associate
        CCP = Child Care Professional

**   A year of employment is defined as a minimum of 1,200 hours (a six-hour workday for an academic year).

The information needed to score this item is obtained from data recorded on the **Teaching Staff Qualifications Worksheet** (page 63) for each group/classroom of children.

1. Determine the total number of Teachers for the entire program and duplicate sufficient copies of Item 24 on page 57 so that each individual designated as a Teacher has a separate Item 24 page.

2. Using the information recorded on the **Teaching Staff Qualifications Worksheet**, rate the indicators for Item 24 for each Teacher.

3. Transfer the individual Teacher Item 24 scores to Column B on the **Summary of Teaching Staff Qualifications** on page 64.

4. Determine the average score for Item 24 by summing the individual Teacher scores and dividing by the number of Teachers. Record this Item 24 Average Score on the bottom of the **Summary of Teaching Staff Qualifications**.

24. Teacher (N/A is allowed)

	1		2		3		4		5		6		7	
	Inadequate				**Minimal**				**Good**				**Excellent**	

___ 1.1   Teacher has less than 30 sh of college credit.

___ 1.2   Teacher does not have a CDA or CCP credential and has less than 6 sh of ECE/CD coursework.*

___ 3.1 D   Teacher has 30 or more sh of college credit.

___ 3.2 D   Teacher has a CDA or CCP credential or 12 or more sh of ECE/CD coursework.*

___ 5.1 D   Teacher has an associate degree or 60 or more sh of college credit.

___ 5.2 D   Teacher has 21or more sh of ECE/CD coursework.

___ 5.3 D   Teacher has one or more years of experience working with young children (birth to 8 years) in a group setting.**

___ 7.1 D   Teacher has 60 or more sh of college credit and is enrolled in a baccalaureate degree program.

___ 7.2 D   Teacher has 30 or more sh of ECE/CD coursework.

___ 7.3 D   Teacher has two or more years of experience working with young children (birth to 8 years) in a group setting.**

Comments:

Circle the final score based on the scoring rules on page 5.

1   2   3   4   5   6   7   N/A

24. Teacher

25. Apprentice Teacher/Aide

Notes	Data Collection Procedure

Notes

An **Apprentice Teacher/Aide** is a member of the teaching team assigned to a group of children who works under the direct supervision of the Lead Teacher and/or Teacher.

Depending on the staffing pattern of the program, there may be more than one person designated as Apprentice Teacher/Aide for each group/classroom of children. It is also possible that a group/classroom of children will not have any assigned Apprentice Teachers/Aides.

Documents needed: **Teaching Staff Qualifications Worksheet**, transcripts, and evidence of teaching experience.

*   A year of employment is defined as a minimum of 1,200 hours (a six-hour workday for an academic year).

Data Collection Procedure

The information needed to score this item is obtained from data recorded on the **Teaching Staff Qualifications Worksheet** (page 63) for each group/classroom of children.

1. Determine the total number of Apprentice Teachers/Aides for the entire program and duplicate sufficient copies of Item 25 on page 59 so that each individual designated as an Apprentice Teacher/Aide has a separate Item 25 page.

2. Using the information recorded on the **Teaching Staff Qualifications Worksheet**, rate the indicators for Item 25 for each Apprentice Teacher/Aide.

3. Transfer the individual Apprentice Teacher/Aide Item 25 scores to Column C on the **Summary of Teaching Staff Qualifications** on page 64.

4. Determine the average score for Item 25 by summing the individual Apprentice Teacher/Aide scores and dividing by the total number of Apprentice Teachers/Aides. Record this Item 25 Average Score on the bottom of the **Summary of Teaching Staff Qualifications.**

25. Apprentice Teacher/Aide (N/A is allowed)

1	2	3	4	5	6	7
Inadequate		**Minimal**		**Good**		**Excellent**

___ 1.1 Apprentice Teacher/Aide does not have a high school diploma or GED.

___ 1.2 Apprentice Teacher/Aide has no college credit in ECE/CD and is not enrolled in ECE/CD coursework.

___ 3.1 Apprentice Teacher/Aide has a
D   high school diploma or GED.

___ 3.2 Apprentice Teacher/Aide has
D   3 or more sh of coursework in ECE/CD **or** is enrolled in ECE/CD coursework.

___ 5.1 Apprentice Teacher/Aide has
D   9 or more sh of college coursework.

___ 5.2 Apprentice Teacher/Aide has
D   6 or more sh of coursework in ECE/CD.

___ 5.3 Apprentice Teacher/Aide
D   has one or more years of supervised experience working with young children (birth to 8 years) in a group setting.*

___ 7.1 Apprentice Teacher/Aide has
D   15 or more sh of college coursework.

___ 7.2 Apprentice Teacher/Aide has
D   9 or more sh of coursework in ECE/CD.

___ 7.3 Apprentice Teacher/Aide has
D   two or more years of supervised experience working with young children (birth to 8 years) in a group setting.*

Comments:

Circle the final score based on the scoring rules on page 5.

1   2   3   4   5   6   7   **N/A**

25. Apprentice Teacher/Aide

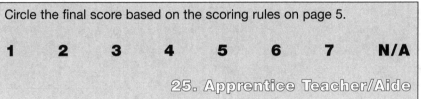

P A S

Program Administration Scale
Worksheets and Forms

- Administrator Qualifications Worksheet

- Teaching Staff Qualifications Worksheet

- Summary of Teaching Qualifications

- Item Summary Form

- PAS Profile

Administrator Qualifications Worksheet

The Administrator is the individual located on-site who is responsible for planning, implementing, and evaluating the early care and education program. This individual's role title might be director, manager, or principal.

Program name: _____   Administrator's name: _____

Highest Education Level

High School/GED ☐
AA/AAS/AAT ☐
BA/BS ☐
MA/MS ☐
PhD ☐

General Education

_____ Total semester hours (sh) of college coursework

Specialized ECE/CD Coursework

_____ Total sh of ECE/CD coursework

Specialized Management Coursework *

_____ Total sh of management coursework

Administrator Credential

Holds administrator credential: ☐ Yes ☐ No

Type/level of credential: _____

Issued by: _____

Management Experience

years _____

months _____

Professional Contributions**

List professional contributions within the last three years:

1._____   4._____

2._____   5._____

3._____   6._____

---

* Examples of management coursework include: accounting, marketing, finance, communications, technology, systems analysis, staff development, and organizational change.

** Professional contributions are activities that show commitment to the field of early childhood beyond center-based responsibilities (e.g., service or leadership in a professional organization, presenting at a professional conference, serving as a resource to media about early childhood issues, mentoring, advocacy, research, publishing, providing training to another program). These activities must be within the last three years.

Teaching Staff Qualifications Worksheet
(Lead Teachers, Teachers, Apprentice Teachers/Aides)

Please complete one worksheet for each group/classroom (see instructions on pages 54, 56, and 58).

Program name: _____   Group/classroom name: _____

Teaching staff initials: ____ ____ ____ ____

Teaching role*: ____ ____ ____ ____

* Teaching Roles:

Lead Teacher
The individual with the highest educational qualifications assigned to teach a group of children and who is responsible for daily lesson planning, parent conferences, child assessment, and curriculum planning.

Teacher
A member of the teaching team who shares responsibility with the Lead Teacher for the care and education of an assigned group of children.

Apprentice Teacher/Aide
A member of the teaching team assigned to a group of children who works under the direct supervision of the Lead Teacher and/or Teacher.

Highest Education Level

	High School/GED	AA/AAS/AAT	BA/BS	MA/MS	PhD
	☐ ☐ ☐ ☐ ☐	☐ ☐ ☐ ☐ ☐	☐ ☐ ☐ ☐ ☐	☐ ☐ ☐ ☐ ☐	

General Education

Total semester hours of college coursework   ____ ____ ____ ____

Specialized Coursework

Total semester hours of ECE/CD coursework   ____ ____ ____ ____

Credentials

CDA
CCP
State Teacher Certification

☐ ☐ ☐   ☐ ☐ ☐   ☐ ☐ ☐   ☐ ☐ ☐

Teaching Experience

years   ____ ____ ____ ____

months   ____ ____ ____ ____

Summary of Teaching Staff Qualifications

Program name: _____ Date: _____

Group/Classroom Name	A Lead Teacher Item 23 Score	B Teacher Item 24 Score	C Apprentice Teacher Item 25 Score
_____	_____	_____ _____ _____	_____ _____ _____
_____	_____	_____ _____	_____ _____
_____	_____	_____ _____ _____	_____ _____ _____
_____	_____	_____ _____ _____	_____ _____ _____
_____	_____	_____ _____ _____	_____ _____ _____

Sum of scores in Column A		Sum of scores in Column B		Sum of scores in Column C	
Number of scores in Column A	÷	Number of scores in Column B	÷	Number of scores in Column C	÷
Item 23 Average Score	=	Item 24 Average Score	=	Item 25 Average Score	=

Item Summary Form

Program name: _____ Date: _____

Instructions

Use this form to summarize the item scores and to calculate the Total PAS Score and Average PAS Item Score.

- Enter the item scores in the space provided.
- Sum all the item scores, and enter the total in the space provided. This is the Total PAS Score.
- Divide the Total PAS Score by the total number of items (minimum of 23 for all programs; 24 or 25 for programs that have a staffing pattern that includes Teachers and/or Apprentice Teachers/Aides). The resulting number is the Average PAS Item Score.

Item	Score
1. Staff Orientation	_____
2. Supervision and Performance Appraisal	_____
3. Staff Development	_____
4. Compensation	_____
5. Benefits	_____
6. Staffing Patterns and Scheduling	_____
7. Facilities Management	_____
8. Risk Management	_____
9. Internal Communications	_____
10. Screening and Identification of Special Needs	_____
11. Assessment in Support of Learning	_____
12. Budget Planning	_____
13. Accounting Practices	_____
14. Program Evaluation	_____
15. Strategic Planning	_____
16. Family Communications	_____
17. Family Support and Involvement	_____
18. External Communications	_____
19. Community Outreach	_____
20. Technological Resources	_____
21. Use of Technology	_____
22. Administrator	_____
23. Lead Teacher	_____
24. Teacher	_____
25. Apprentice Teacher/Aide	_____

Sum of item scores

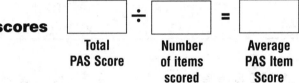

$$\boxed{} \div \boxed{} = \boxed{}$$

Total PAS Score   Number of items scored   Average PAS Item Score

The Program Administration Scale (PAS)
Profile

Program name: _____   Date: _____

Subscales	Items	1	2	3	4	5	6	7
Human Resources Development	1. Staff Orientation							
	2. Supervision and Performance Appraisal							
	3. Staff Development							
Personnel Cost and Allocation	4. Compensation							
	5. Benefits							
	6. Staffing Patterns and Scheduling							
Center Operations	7. Facilities Management							
	8. Risk Management							
	9. Internal Communications							
Child Assessment	10. Screening and Identification of Special Needs							
	11. Assessment in Support of Learning							
Fiscal Management	12. Budget Planning							
	13. Accounting Practices							
Program Planning and Evaluation	14. Program Evaluation							
	15. Strategic Planning							
Family Partnerships	16. Family Communications							
	17. Family Support and Involvement							
Marketing and Public Relations	18. External Communications							
	19. Community Outreach							
Technology	20. Technological Resources							
	21. Use of Technology							
Staff Qualifications	22. Administrator							
	23. Lead Teacher							
	24. Teacher							
	25. Apprentice Teacher/Aide							

Total PAS Score ————— ÷ **Number of items** ————— = **Average PAS Item Score** —————

Program Administration Scale

Appendices

- Psychometric Characteristics of the PAS

- References and Resources

- About the Authors

Psychometric Characteristics of the PAS

Psychometric Criteria

The development of the *Program Administration Scale* was guided by seven psychometric criteria:

1. The PAS should measure distinct but related administrative practices of an early childhood program.
2. The PAS should be able to differentiate low- and high-quality programs.
3. The PAS should be applicable for use in different types of programs (e.g., for-profit, nonprofit, part-day, full-day, faith-based, military, Head Start, corporate-sponsored).
4. The PAS should be applicable for use in programs of varying sizes.
5. The PAS should demonstrate good internal consistency among scale items.
6. The PAS should demonstrate good inter-rater reliability.
7. The PAS should be easy to score and generate an easy-to-understand profile to support program improvement efforts.

Sample

A reliability and validity study of the *Program Administration Scale* was conducted from May to December 2003 involving 67 center-based early childhood programs. Data generated from the reliability and validity study were used to make revisions in the wording of different indicators, delete redundant items, and streamline the data-collection protocol.

The sample for the PAS reliability and validity study was drawn from early care and education programs in Illinois. The Illinois Network of Child Care Resource and Referral Agencies (INCCRRA) generated a list of all child care centers in Cook (Chicago), Cook (Suburban), Jackson, Madison, McLean, and Winnebago counties with contact information and descriptive data on center capacity, NAEYC-accreditation status, and legal auspices. The counties targeted for the pilot were selected because they included urban, suburban, and rural geographic regions of the state.

The Metropolitan Chicago Information Center (MCIC) took the INCCRRA information and constructed a sample frame based on the center's NAEYC-accreditation status (not accredited and accredited) and center size (small, medium, large). From this pool, MCIC drew a random sample of 120 centers in six cells. The sample was examined for geographic distribution. An additional 56 centers were randomly selected and added to the pool to ensure adequate representation of each of the geographic areas.

From the total pool of 176 programs, 124 centers were randomly contacted and asked to participate in the PAS reliability and validity study. A total of 67 centers agreed to participate and interviews with the on-site administrator were scheduled. As Table 1 depicts, participating centers included an adequate representation of small, medium, and large programs as well as NAEYC-accredited and not-accredited programs.

Table 1. Distribution of the Sample by Size and Accreditation Status (N = 67)

Accreditation Status	Center Size						Total	
	small		medium		large			
	n	%	n	%	n	%	n	%
Not Accredited	8	12	15	22	12	18	35	52
Accredited	7	10	14	21	11	17	32	48
Total	**15**	**22**	**29**	**43**	**23**	**35**	**67**	**100**

Note: small = < 51 children; medium = 51–100 children; large = > 100 children
NAEYC accreditation was used to determine accreditation status

The mean licensed capacity of centers included in the sample was 102 children. Centers employed on average 17 staff who worked more than ten hours per week. Table 2 is a distribution of centers by program type. Approximately two-thirds of the programs were nonprofit; one-third were from the for-profit sector. Twenty-two of the programs in the nonprofit sector received Head Start funding and five programs in the sample were sponsored by faith-based organizations.

Table 2. Distribution of the Sample by Program Type (N = 67)

Program Type	n	%
Nonprofit – part of agency or organization	31	46
Nonprofit – independent	14	21
For-profit – private proprietary or partnership	6	9
For-profit – corporation or chain (e.g., Kindercare, Children's World)	10	15
For-profit – corporate sponsored (e.g., Bright Horizons Family Solutions)	6	9
Total	**67**	**100**

Reliability and Validity

Content validity. Content validity for the *Program Administration Scale* was established by a panel of ten early childhood experts who evaluated each indicator, item, and subscale on the PAS to ensure that key leadership and management practices of center-based early childhood programs were included. Content reviewers were asked to respond to the following questions and provide feedback:

- Do the items under each subscale adequately describe the subscale?
- Do the indicators under each item adequately represent each item?
- Do the indicators appropriately show increasing levels of quality on a continuum?
- Does the wording of the item and subscale headings adequately reflect their content?

In addition to the content evaluation by ten early childhood experts, the *Program Administration Scale* was also reviewed informally by ten other early childhood administrators, consultants, and trainers. Multiple refinements were made to the wording and layout of the PAS as a result of the insightful feedback received from reviewers. Additional revisions were made from feedback received from the assessors who visited the 67 programs and interviewed the directors and from the MCIC statisticians involved in the data analysis. As a result, the wording of several indicators was changed to be more applicable to the full range of early childhood program type, auspice, and size.

Descriptive statistics. Table 3 provides the mean scores and standard deviations for the 25 items rated using the 7-point scale of the PAS. There are a total of 79 indicator strands used to compute scores for the 25

Table 3. Mean Scores and Standard Deviations for PAS Items (N = 67)

Item #	Item	Indicator Strands	M	S.D.
Human Resources Development				
1	Staff orientation	3	3.50	2.22
2	Supervision/performance appraisal	3	4.07	1.96
3	Staff development	3	3.16	1.94
Personnel Cost and Allocation				
4	Compensation	3	1.96	1.56
5	Benefits	5	3.13	2.24
6	Staffing patterns and scheduling	4	2.88	2.40
Center Operations				
7	Facilities management	3	4.91	1.80
8	Risk management	4	3.09	1.82
9	Internal communications	5	2.45	1.86
Child Assessment				
10	Screening/identification of special needs	2	3.43	2.62
11	Assessment in support of learning	2	4.21	2.25
Fiscal Management				
12	Budget planning	3	3.42	4.30
13	Accounting practices	3	3.76	2.46
Program Planning and Evaluation				
14	Program evaluation	3	3.72	2.53
15	Strategic planning	2	2.30	2.02
Family Partnerships				
16	Family communications	4	4.48	2.36
17	Family support and involvement	3	5.52	1.65
Marketing and Public Relations				
18	External communications	3	4.34	1.83
19	Community outreach	3	3.22	2.20
Staff Qualifications				
20	Technological resources	2	4.72	2.13
21	Use of technology	3	4.03	2.15
Technology				
22	Administrator	4	2.58	1.84
23	Lead Teacher	3	3.11	1.28
24	Teacher*	3	3.92	1.41
25	Apprentice Teacher/Aide**	3	3.77	1.59
	Total PAS	**79**	**89.68**	**22.41**

* n = 26; ** n = 31

The Total PAS Score is the sum of the item scores. Because the 10 subscales of the PAS are used only as convenient headings for clustering items, and not as separate indicators of organizational effectiveness, mean scores for the subscales are not included on the profile that users generate to guide their program improvement efforts.

The average Total PAS Score for the reliability and validity sample was 89.68 for the 25 items. The average PAS Item Score for all items was 3.59 with 29% of items rated at a level 1 and 13% rated at a level 7. This suggests that the PAS has an acceptable distribution of item scores across the quality continuum. It should be noted that the 67 programs participating in the pilot did not receive a copy of the instrument prior to the administration of the scale by a trained assessor. It is anticipated that as the PAS is used broadly, the percentage of programs being rated at a level 1 on items will decrease as on-site administrators will be better prepared with the necessary documentation for each indicator.

Internal consistency. The degree of coherence of items included on the *Program Administration Scale*, its internal consistency, was determined through computation of Cronbach's Alpha coefficient. Coefficient alpha for the total scale was .85, indicating that the PAS has acceptable internal consistency among items.

Distinctiveness of the subscales. The 10 subscales were correlated to determine the extent to which they measured distinct, though somewhat related, aspects of early childhood administration. Table 4 reports the results of the Pearson's r correlational analysis. Subscale intercorrelations range from .09 to .63, with a median value of .33, confirming that the subscales, for the most part, measure distinct characteristics of organizational administration.

Table 4. Subscale Intercorrelations

Subscale	2	3	4	5	6	7	8	9	10
1. Human resources development	.39	.41	.27	.47	.44	.63	.33	.42	.21
2. Personnel cost/allocation		.33	.46	.47	.47	.53	.19	.25	.23
3. Center operations			.13	.26	.48	.52	.32	.27	.30
4. Child assessment				.20	.35	.30	.09	.11	.12
5. Fiscal management					.33	.39	.35	.49	.13
6. Program planning/evaluation						.62	.26	.38	.26
7. Family partnerships							.28	.42	.24
8. Marketing/public relations								.20	.08
9. Technology									.21
10. Staff qualifications									--

Item intercorrelations were also calculated using Pearson's r. These coefficients ranged from .02 to .78 confirming that the individual items on the PAS also measure somewhat distinct but related characteristics of organizational administration.

Inter-rater reliability. Inter-rater reliability, the degree to which the assessor's item scores match the PAS anchor's scores, was determined during a two-day training on the use of the instrument with eight early childhood assessors. Using a videotape of the entire interview protocol, assessors were rated on how often they matched the PAS anchor's scores within 1 point for each item. Individual assessor's inter-rater reliability scores ranged from 81% to 95% agreement on the 25 items. Overall inter-rater reliability was 90% for the eight assessors used in the PAS pilot.

Differentiating programs. In order to determine if the *Program Administration Scale* adequately differentiates programs of varying quality, analysis of variance procedures were employed. NAEYC accreditation status was used as a measure of program quality. Those programs that were currently accredited by NAEYC were presumed to be of higher quality than those that were not accredited. Analysis of variance offers an empirical test of whether the PAS can differentiate programs based on their accreditation status.

Table 5 provides a summary of the analysis of varience (ANOVA). The results provide confirmatory evidence that the PAS can adequately differentiate programs based on level of quality. Those programs that were accredited had significantly higher Total PAS Scores (M = 92.12, S.D. = 19.43) than those that were not accredited (M = 72.06, S.D. = 20.83). The Total PAS Scores for this analysis were based on 23 items (possible range 23–161) since all centers did not include the positions of Teacher and Apprentice Teacher/Aide on the teaching staff.

Table 5. Analysis of Variance by Accreditation Status

	Sum of Squares	df	Mean Square	F	p <
Between groups	6740.36	1	6740.36	16.59	.0001
Within groups	26411.40	65	406.33		
Total	33151.76	66			

Table 6 reports the rank ordering of specific items that were found to be most strongly associated with accreditation status. As noted in this table *family communications*, *lead teacher qualifications*, and *program evaluation* differed the most with regard to accreditation status.

Table 6. Items Most Strongly Associated with Accreditation Status (N = 67)

Item	Not accredited M	Accredited M	p <
Family communications	3.16	5.59	.001
Lead Teacher qualifications	2.40	4.49	.001
Program evaluation	2.52	4.59	.001
Use of technology	3.13	4.48	.01
Budget planning	2.58	4.00	.01
Assessment in support of learning	3.32	4.79	.01
Compensation	1.58	2.52	.02
Staffing patterns/scheduling	1.65	2.69	.03
Supervision/performance appraisal	3.39	4.41	.03

Additional analyses were conducted to ensure that the *Program Administration Scale* did not unfairly discriminate against programs of different sizes. For 23 of the 25 items there were no statistically significant differences in PAS scores based on program size (small = < 50 children; medium = 51–100 children; large = >100 children). For the 67 programs included in the pilot, the item *staffing patterns and scheduling* had higher scores in smaller programs and the item *accounting practices* had higher scores in larger programs (p < .05).

Concurrent validity. Concurrent validity for the PAS was determined by a correlational analysis with two other instruments that measure early childhood organizational effectiveness: the Opportunities for Professional Growth subscale of the *Early Childhood Work Environment Survey* (Bloom, 1996a) and the Parents and Staff subscale of the *Early Childhood Environment Rating Scale–Revised* (Harms, Clifford, & Cryer, 1998). As Table 7 shows, the moderate correlations with both the ECERS-R and ECWES indicate that the PAS measures related but not redundant characteristics of organizational quality.

Table 7. Correlation of PAS Subscales with the ECERS-R Parents and Staff Subscale and the ECWES Professional Growth Subscale (N = 67)

PAS Subscale	ECERS-R	ECWES
Human resources development	.33	.42
Personnel cost and allocation	.45	.42
Center operations	.33	.32
Child assessment	.29	.05
Fiscal management	.47	.40
Program planning and evaluation	.36	.24
Family partnerships	.34	.43
Marketing and public relations	.10	.05
Technology	.32	.38
Staff qualifications	.26	.35
PAS Total	**.53**	**.52**

The results of the reliability and validity study support the conclusion that the *Program Administration Scale* has achieved all seven psychometric criteria: It measures somewhat distinct but related administrative practices of early childhood programs, can differentiate between low- and high-quality programs as measured by NAEYC-accreditation status, is applicable for use in different types of programs, does not unfairly discriminate against programs of varying sizes, demonstrates good internal consistency, has good inter-rater reliability, and is easy to score and use as a tool to support program improvement efforts.

References and Resources

Abbott-Shim, M., & Sibley, A. (1997). *Assessment Profile for Early Childhood Programs.* Atlanta, GA: Quality Assist.

Barnett, W. S., Robin, K. B., Hustedt, J. T., & Schulman, K. L. (2003). *The state of preschool: 2003 state preschool yearbook.* New Brunswick, NJ: National Institute for Early Education Research.

Bertachi, J. (1996, October/November). Relationship-based organizations. *Zero to Three Bulletin, 17*(2), 2–7.

Bloom, P. J. (1989). *The 1989 Illinois Directors' Study.* Springfield: Illinois Department of Children and Family Services.

Bloom, P. J. (1996a). *Improving the quality of work life in the early childhood setting: Resource guide and technical manual for the Early Childhood Work Environment Survey.* Wheeling, IL: McCormick Tribune Center for Early Childhood Leadership, National-Louis University.

Bloom, P. J. (1996b). The quality of work life in NAEYC accredited and non-accredited early childhood programs. *Early Education and Development, 7*(4), 301–317.

Bloom, P. J. (2000). *Circle of influence: Implementing shared decision making and participative management.* Lake Forest, IL: New Horizons.

Bloom, P. J. (2003). *Leadership in action: How effective directors get things done.* Lake Forest, IL: New Horizons.

Bowman, B., Donovan, M. S., & Burns, M. S. (Eds.). (2001). *Eager to learn: Educating our preschoolers.* Washington, DC: National Academy Press.

Burchinal, M., Cryer, D., Clifford, R., & Howes, C. (2002). Caregiver training and classroom quality in child care centers. *Applied Developmental Science, 6*(1), 2–11.

Center for the Child Care Workforce. (1998). *Creating better child care jobs: Model work standards.* Washington, DC: Author.

Cost, Quality, and Child Outcomes Study Team. (1995). *Cost, quality, and child outcomes in child care centers.* Denver: Department of Economics, University of Colorado at Denver.

Dahlberg, G., Moss, P., & Pence, A. (1999). *Beyond quality in early childhood education and care: Postmodern perspectives.* London: Falmer Press.

Espinosa, L. M. (2002, November). High-quality preschool: Why we need it and what it looks like. *Preschool Policy Matters, 1*(1), 1–10.

Family Support America. (2001). *Family support and child care.* Chicago: Author.

Governor's Task Force on Universal Preschool. (2002). *Ready, set, grow: Illinois preschool.* Springfield, IL: Author.

Harms, T., Clifford, R., & Cryer, D. (1998). *Early Childhood Environment Rating Scale–Revised.* New York: Teachers College Press.

Harms, T., Cryer, D., & Clifford, R. (2003). *Infant/Toddler Environment Rating Scale–Revised.* New York: Teachers College Press.

References and Resources

Helm, J. H. (2002). *Best practices in early childhood assessment.* Presentation at Early Childhood Symposium, Community Consolidated School District 65, Evanston, Illinois, October 26.

Hemmeter, M. L., Joseph, G. E., Smith, B. J., & Sandall, S. (Eds.). (2001). *DEC recommended practices program assessment: Improving practices for young children with special needs and their families.* Longmont, CO: Sopris West.

High/Scope Educational Research Foundation. (2003). *Preschool Program Quality Assessment (PQA).* Ypsilanti, MI: Author.

Hyun, E. (1998). *Making sense of developmentally and culturally appropriate practice (DCAP) in early childhood education.* New York: Peter Lang.

Illinois Network of Child Care Resource and Referral Agencies. (1999). *The Illinois Director Credential.* Bloomington, IL: Author.

Kagan, S. L., & Bowman, B. (Eds.). (1997). *Leadership in early care and education.* Washington, DC: National Association for the Education of Young Children.

Malaguzzi, L. (1993). For an education based on relationships. *Young Children, 49*(1), 9–12.

National Association for the Education of Young Children. (1998). *Accreditation criteria and procedures of the National Association for the Education of Young Children.* Washington, DC: Author.

Phillips, D., Mekos, D., Scarr, S., McCartney, K., & Abbott-Shim, M. (2000). Within and beyond the classroom door: Assessing quality in child care centers. *Early Childhood Research Quarterly, 15*(4), 475–496.

Scarr, S., Eisenberg, M., & Deata-Deckard, K. (1994). Measurements of quality in child care centers. *Early Childhood Research Quarterly, 9,* 131–151.

Shepard, L., Kagan, S. L., & Wurtz, E. (Eds.). (1998). *Principles and recommendations for early childhood assessments.* Washington, DC: National Education Goals Panel.

Vandell, D. L., & Wolfe, B. (2000). *Child care quality: Does it matter and does it need to be improved?* Madison: Institute for Research on Poverty, University of Wisconsin.

Whitebook, M. (2003). *Early education quality: Higher teacher qualifications for better learning environments.* Berkeley, CA: Institute of Industrial Relations, Center for the Study of Child Care Employment.

Whitebook, M., Howes, C., & Phillips, D. (1990). *Who cares? Child care teachers and the quality of care in America: Final report of the National Child Care Staffing Study.* Oakland, CA: Child Care Employee Project.

Work/Family Directions. (2000). *Family-friendly audit tool for child care centers.* Watertown, MA: Author.

About the Authors

Teri N. Talan, M.Ed., J.D.

Teri N. Talan is Director of Research and Public Policy for the McCormick Tribune Center for Early Childhood Leadership and Assistant Professor of Early Childhood Education at National-Louis University in Wheeling, Illinois. She represents the Center in public policy forums and promotes action by state and national policymakers on early childhood education and program administration issues. She is also the editor of the Center's quarterly *Research Notes*. Previously, Ms. Talan was the Executive Director of an NAEYC-accredited early childhood program. She holds a law degree from Northwestern University and an M.Ed. in Early Childhood Leadership and Advocacy from National-Louis University. Ms. Talan's research interests are in the areas of workforce development, systems integration, and program quality evaluation. She is co-author of the publication, *Who's Caring for the Kids? The Status of the Early Childhood Workforce in Illinois.*

Paula Jorde Bloom, Ph.D.

Paula Jorde Bloom is the Michael W. Louis Chair of the McCormick Tribune Center for Early Childhood Leadership and Professor of Early Childhood Education at National-Louis University in Wheeling, Illinois. As one of the country's leading experts on early childhood leadership and program management issues, Dr. Bloom is a frequent keynote speaker at state, national, and international conferences and consultant to professional organizations and state agencies. She received her master's and doctoral degrees from Stanford University. She is the author of numerous journal articles and several widely read books including *Avoiding Burnout, A Great Place to Work, Blueprint for Action, Circle of Influence, Making the Most of Meetings, Workshop Essentials,* and *Leadership in Action.* Dr. Bloom's research interests are in the areas of organizational climate, occupational stress, job satisfaction, staff development, professional orientation, and other early childhood workforce issues. She is the author of the *Early Childhood Work Environment Survey* (ECWES) and the *Early Childhood Job Satisfaction Survey* (ECJSS).